Swansea City Football Club

1. The Preston goalkeeper is beaten by this curling shot from Leighton James to set Swansea on the way to victory and the First Division in the promotion decider at Deepdale.

John Burgum

First published 1988 by

Archive Publications Ltd
Carrington Business Park
Urmston
Manchester
M31 4DD

in association with

South Wales Evening Post
The Swansea Press Ltd
P O Box 14
Adelaide Street
Swansea
SA1 1QT

Production by Richardson Press

© 1988 copyright text John Burgum
© 1988 copyright photographs South Wales Evening Post and others as listed
© 1988 copyright arrangement Archive Publications Ltd

ISBN: 0-948946-19-9

2. John Toshack powers a header over the desperate hands of Spurs goalkeeper Barry Daines to put Swansea on the way to a giant-killing performance in the League Cup replay at White Hart Lane in 1978.

CONTENTS

Foreword
by
Doug Sharpe

Most people see me purely and simply as chairman of Swansea City, but I am today what I've always been - a supporter.

Unlike the Swansea players I've been privileged to watch over the years my flirtation with the game never got beyond local football. I did make the 1953-54 Swansea schoolboy squad as a goalkeeper and played in the same side as Herbie Williams who served the club so loyally over many ' 'er I played for local teams in the Senior League and Welsh League, but my heart was 'ch Field, so much so that I frequently used to run to matches on a Saturday afternoon League game.

Swans has been a big part of my life, and one of my favourite stories concerns the 196. up run when Swansea reached the semi-finals. I was at Villa Park when the TV camer .ed up a Swansea fan running around the pitch at the end of the game wearing a steel helmet with the words "Up the Swans" written on it. That was me and I've still got the helmet to prove i

I've been on the board since 1980 and I've been chairman twice, but I've never forgotten my roots. The only difference today is that I get to see life behind the scenes. Over the past few years that extra involvement has had its traumatic moments, not least when the club was threatened with closure. Life would not have been the same without the Swans, and I'm glad I was able to play a significant part in keeping the club alive.

Now things are improving again, and I'm glad that a book like this one has been produced covering the first 75 years. I say the "first" because I hope to get many, many more years of enjoyment watching my favourite team.

Doug Sharpe
Chairman
Swansea City

Birth and Marriage

Soccer in Swansea, traditional rugby country, can be traced back to the 1870s, but progress was slow until the game was fostered in local schools.

In 1900 former schoolboy players banded together to form the Swansea and District League and by 1909 interest had grown to such an extent that there was hope of organising a senior club for the town.

The chief obstacle was the availability of a central ground which was resolved in 1912 when Vetch Field became available. The Swansea Gaslight Company had failed to gain Parliamentary permission to develop the site following stiff opposition from the Sandfields residents. The area had been used by local sportsmen for some time but had never been grassed.

Enthusiasm was such that at a public meeting on 14 June 1912 at the Royal Hotel, a professional club was founded and Mr J W Thorpe, a Swansea solicitor and clerk to Pontardawe Justices, became the first chairman.

The board of directors comprised businessmen with a keen interest in the game: Mr Harry Behenna, a coal exporter; Councillor Percy Molineux, a fish merchant; Mr Frank Newcombe; Mr Tom Martin, of the Terminus Hotel; Mr Trevor Hopkins; Mr D J Bassett; and Mr S B Williams, who was appointed secretary.

Armed with a seven year lease and great determination the club went about preparing both the team and the ground for the coming season, and by September 1912 all was ready.

Goalkeeper-manager Walter Whittaker hurriedly got together a squad of twenty players: Davidson, Ball, Swarbrick, Sutherland, Grierson, Jepp, Nicholas, Duffy, Coleman, Cleverly, Hamilton, Messer, Davies, Prideaux, Soady, Fisher, Anthony, Fyfe, Anderson and Weir. They were now ready to compete both in the Welsh League and the Second Division of the Southern League.

The first competitive game was against Cardiff and Swansea took the field with Whittaker, Cleverly, Nicholas, Duffy, Hamilton, Jepp, Messer, Coleman, Ball, Grierson, and Swarbrick. It ended in a 1-1 draw with hero of the day, Billy Ball, scoring the first goal for the club. Ball went on to become the first player to score a hat-trick and, the following season, was the first Swansea player to be sent off, albeit for a minor offence. He was a great favourite with the crowd: "Give it to Bally" was a frequent cry from the terraces. The fans even sang a song about him and another Swansea favourite, full-back Jack Nicholas.

Swansea had a hugely successful first season -

3. Double winners ... the first team roll call complete with Welsh Cup and Welsh Championship Trophy. 1912

they finished third in the Southern League and beat Pontypridd to lift the Welsh Cup. It was a remarkable achievement for a new club and the whole town shared in the excitement when the Cup was triumphantly paraded through the streets.

In the opening match of the following season Swansea clinched the Welsh League Championship held over from the previous campaign and Ball scored a hat-trick.

New drainage and a grass pitch meant players no longer needed kneepads as protection against the cinder surface but the softer ground made little difference when 18,000 poured in to watch the FA Cup tie against Queens Park Rangers which Swansea lost 2-1.

Kaiser Bill was already flexing his muscles for a different kind of confrontation when the 1913-14 season ended. Swansea were runners-up in the Welsh League, fourth in the Southern League and beaten semi-finalists in the Welsh Cup in circumstances which would not occur today. On the same day that they played Llanelli, the club also had to play a Southern League fixture.

By the time the new season started Whittaker had been sacked. New manager John William Bartlett brought in newcomers Storey, Allman, Cubberly, Bassett, Greer, Mayo and Jack Williams. Jock Weir, signed on loan from Fulham, was in the 1913 Welsh Cup final line-up.

With the outbreak of war, fixtures seemed uncertain. Rugby was abandoned immediately but, as conscription had not been introduced, the Football Association decided to continue, despite a feeling among Press and public that it was unpatriotic.

Vetch Field was offered to the military and, for a time, was used to accommodate the horses of the 1st Welsh Howitzers when the club were not playing. A full programme was needed to maintain the necessary income and Swansea benefitted from the absence of the rival rugby code by the arrival of the talented Ben Beynon, who was an accomplished rugby player too young for military service. Originally an amateur soccer player he played rugby for the All Whites until the outbreak of war when he joined Swansea Town as an amateur. After hostilities ceased, he returned to rugby where he was capped by Wales. He later returned to play professionally for Swansea Town before transferring to Oldham Athletic. He also played rugby league at Oldham before ending his varied career at Vetch Field in 1926.

One of the highlights of Beynon's career was the winning goal he scored for Swansea against Football League Champions Blackburn Rovers in an FA Cup tie in January 1915.

Swansea's success was shortlived. In the next round they went out to Newcastle after a replay. The first match at St. James' Park was the first Cup tie, other than a final, to use extra time on the day of its introduction.

The restrictions and problems brought about by the war resulted in many resignations, and the six goals scored by Weir against Leyton in September 1914 were scratched from the records when Leyton were disbanded. Finally, on 19 April 1915, the football authorities yielded to the growing pressure and announced that there would be no more League and Cup matches until the war was over. The news was greeted with relief by most professional clubs. Many were on the brink of bankruptcy. With a weekly wage bill of £60 Swansea's success in the FA Cup brought in much needed income. The club was kept afloat by a local League based at factories making munitions while charity matches contributed to war funds. A number of Swansea players left to fight in the trenches. Some, like Bulcock and Mitchell, did not return.

After the war the club had to be almost completely rebuilt. New chairman B Watts-Jones had kept things ticking over, ensuring that the ground was maintained and the club remained solvent.

In January 1919 the new-look Southern League First Division was extended to twenty-two clubs and after considerable lobbying Swansea joined the elite band.

Among the new players were Evan Jones, a Welsh international from Bolton, and winger Billy Hole, a local youngster soon to follow Jones into the national side. Joe Bradshaw, manager of Southend until the outbreak of war, barely had time to get out

"BILLY" HOLE. IVOR JONES.
WELSH INTERNATIONALS.
SWANSEA TOWN AFC 1919-20

4. Two more firsts: Billy Hole (*left*) who scored the first international goal at Vetch Field, and Ivor Jones, Swansea's first senior international.

of uniform before being appointed Swansea's new manager.

He had to work fast to lick his new team into shape. Ernie Edwards, who had built a fine reputation at Burnley, was appointed trainer, and Jack Nicholas, the club's prewar captain, returned as player-coach. Several new players were brought in, among them Jock Denoon, a goalkeeper from QPR.

The start of the 1919-20 season was disappointing and frustrating. Swansea could not score goals and W Y Brown was signed in an effort to remedy the situation.

It began to improve steadily before tragedy struck. Tich Evans, one of the stars of the team, committed suicide at Vetch Field in a severe state of depression over the death of his young wife. His death cast a shadow over the club and for the first time Swansea failed to qualify for the first round of the FA Cup.

A few months later Beynon, at the peak of his amateur rugby career, signed professional forms for the Swans along with Joe Spottiswood, an outside left from Chelsea who played almost two hundred games over six seasons. In January 1920, Ivor Jones was capped against Ireland - the first of many Swansea players to represent their country while with the club.

After a poor start the club finished ninth in the Southern League, but that was just a foretaste of what was to come. The Football League introduced a Third Division for the 1920-21 season and Swansea, together with Merthyr and Newport, were among its founder members.

5. Rugby convert Ben Beynon played rugby union, rugby league and soccer.

6. One of the first team photographs, complete with young mascot and furry friend held by Billy Ball.

7-9. *above left:* Billy Ball scored the first competitive goal and had the dubious distinction of becoming the first Swansea player to be sent off. *centre:* Jack Nicholas, 1912-20, one of the early club captains. His son (also named Jack) played as an amateur for Swansea until signing professional forms with Derby County during the 1928-29 season. *right:* David Anderson, 1912-15.

10. The smart set ... Swansea players in the casual dress of the day before the FA Cup tie against Blackburn in January 1915. *from left to right:* Ivor Brown, Owen Evans, director, Bert Gilboy, Ben Beynon, David Anderson, Jack Duffy, Amos Lloyd, Ben Hurst, Harry Read, Joe Bulcock, Jack Hewitt, manager of the Langland Bay Hotel, Charlie Lock and W Wishart, trainer.

THE VETCH FIELD AS IT WILL BE.

The above is a sketch of the Swansea Town Association Football Ground—the Vetch Field—as it will be. It is, however, intended to proceed with the work by instalments, and, as exclusively announced in the "Leader" last week, the erection of the grand stand, which is on the reader's left, will be the first to be erected. Tenders are out for the erection of a portion of this stand to seat about 1,000, and it will be built in such a way as will allow additions to be made from time to time. The above sketch was made by a "Leader" artist from a drawing by Mr. Benj. Jones, architect and surveyor, Wind-street, Swansea.

12. Jack Duffy, 1912-15.

13. Frank Mayo, 1913-14.

14. Ivor Brown, 1913-20.

15. S Bassett, 1913-14.

16. E Storey, 1913-14.

17. J B Crumley, 1919-20.

TICH EVANS.

Swansea Football Sensation.

FOUND WITH HIS THROAT CUT.

In the whole annals of Swansea sport no such tragic occurrence has been reported as that which occurred on Thursday at the Vetch Field, Swansea, when "Tich" Evans's body was found underneath the grand stand with his head almost severed, and a razor in his hand.

The discovery was made by Jack Nicholas early in the afternoon, and the police were immediately communicated with.

"Tich," it was well known, had been very depressed ever since the death of his young wife, three weeks ago. He was devoted to her, and despite the many endeavours of his colleagues to infuse some spirit into him, he had been dejected ever since.

On Saturday last he played against Brentford, but he was not the old sparkling "Tich."

On Thursday morning he put in an appearance on the Vetch, but when the rest of the players went out for their morning's training he was missing, and at 12 o'clock, when the players returned to the dressing room, there was still no sign of him. His absence was reported to Mr. Joe Bradshaw, the manager, and a messenger was sent up to the player's lodgings. At 2 o'clock, however, Mr. Bradshaw was informed that "Tich" had not been home to dinner.

When the players re-assembled after dinner "Tich" was still absent, but no one thought that he had met with so tragic a fate. Jack Nicholas eventually had occasion to go under the grand stand, when in a corner, near the players' entrance, he made the terrible discovery.

He had evidently been dead for some time, and there was a huge gash in the throat, whilst in his hand was clutched a blood-stained razor. The police were immediately informed, and the body removed.

He leaves an aged widowed mother, who resides at Barry.

18. How the *Leader* reported the tragic death of Tich Evans in December 1919.

Roaring Twenties

Once Swansea's League pioneers had come to terms with the tougher competitive demands of the Football League, marriage evidently agreed with the club.

Within six seasons Swansea had lifted the Third Division Championship, winning promotion to the Second Division where they remained for twenty-two years. They also reached the semi-final of the FA Cup.

At the start, though, it was a struggle despite the arrival of new players like Wilf Milne and Joe Edmunson from Sheffield Wednesday. Milne, famous for his sliding tackle, went on to make club history with a record 585 League appearances, while Edmunson finished as top scorer in the first League season with 23 goals.

Initially results were poor - Swansea lost the first League match 3-0 at Portsmouth on 28 August 1920 - and the team struggled near the foot of the table. Supporters still flocked to the ground in their thousands and they were rewarded with a four-month run of success which featured outstanding performances from Beynon, Brown, Ivor Jones and Hole.

At the end of October the club was almost bottom. By Easter they were in the running for promotion but eventually had to settle for fifth place despite nine away wins - a record which would stand until 1987-88.

Financially it was a record season and at the end

of it Ivor Jones and Billy Hole were capped against Ireland with Hole, on his Wales debut, scoring the first international goal at Vetch Field.

Two new faces were added to the side for the following season: full back Ernie Morley, and Willie Davies who was signed in exchange for a donation of 10s 6d to Rhymney.

With Brown taking over the captaincy, hopes were high, but despite a record 8-1 win over Bristol Rovers, with Brown and Jimmy Collins scoring hat-tricks, Swansea never recovered from a sluggish start and finished tenth. On top of that Ivor Jones was sold to West Bromwich for a record £2,500. Supporters did not take kindly to losing one of their favourites, and the tide of despondency swept away the old board. Mr J W Thorpe, the club's founding chairman, took over the reins and Bradshaw was given the go-ahead to sign twelve new players. They included John Harwood, Harry Deacon, an inside forward from Birmingham, Joe Roulson, a half back also from Birmingham, Len Thompson and John Smith, a centre forward who cost £250 from Queen's Park Rangers.

Smith, taking over from Beynon, proved an instant success, but although he emerged as top scorer with 23 goals Swansea could only finish third at the end of the 1922-23 season despite scoring 78 goals, more than any other club in the Football League.

By the start of the 1923-24 season Swansea had

19. League pioneers ... the Swansea staff at the start of that 1920-21 season.

embarked on a tour of Denmark, the first Welsh club to play abroad. Nearer home changes saw the departure of Edmunson, Crumley and McCullum but there was renewed optimism under new chairman Mr Owen Evans, and it proved well founded. By Christmas Swansea led the table by five points but the season turned sour after the club lost a Cup tie to Aston Villa following a controversial refereeing decision.

Somehow Swansea never fully recovered and by the time Jack Fowler arrived from Plymouth in a transfer deal which cost the club £1,280, the season was all but over. Fowler quickly made an impression alongside Davies, Deacon, Thompson, Spottiswood and Hole, but Swansea could do no better than fourth. The arrival of Fowler proved a significant turning point and by the time half back Joe Sykes arrived from Sheffield Wednesday, Swansea had the nucleus of a side able to stay the course. Sykes took over the captaincy and after a jittery start to the 1924-25 season, Swansea hit top form when they whipped Charlton 6-1 with Fowler scoring five of the goals. By Christmas Swansea were leading the table again and this time they stayed there to lift the Third Division Championship. Just for good measure the club won the Welsh League and Southern League titles as well.

The Championship squad which made it a triple triumph comprised Denoon, Robson, Bennett, Lamb, Milne, Morley, Langford, Collins, Bellamy, Sykes, McPherson, Booth, Humphries, Davies, Hole, Deacon, Fowler, Thompson, Spottiswood, Corkindale, Whitehead, Lewis, Holland, Miller, Nicholas, Thomas, Logie, Woods, Handley and Williams.

Success spilled over into the following season when Swansea finished fifth in the Second Division and reached the semi-finals of the FA Cup after defeating Exeter, Watford, Blackpool, Stoke, Millwall and Arsenal. But they met their match in Bolton who scored three times in the first 25 minutes of the semi-final and went on to lift the trophy.

Fowler top scored for the second successive season but Swansea missed a glorious opportunity to build on the success of the previous two campaigns. Manager Bradshaw left for domestic reasons and when he was not replaced morale dropped - so did the team, top at the end of November, twelfth when the season ended.

New manager James H Thompson was appointed in time to accompany the team on a close season tour of Spain and Portugal where the club played 'unknown' local sides including Real Madrid and Benfica.

Denoon, who had played almost 200 games, was not retained for the following season when plans were drawn up for a double-decker stand, the first of its kind in Wales, to seat 2,120.

Despite the exciting play provided by Lachlan McPherson, Fowler, Hole and Lewis, who scored a remarkable 43 goals in 64 League games, Swansea were no longer the force they used to be and the problems deepened when Thompson was sold to Arsenal. Swansea still finished sixth in the 1927-28 season, largely through the goal scoring efforts of top marksman Lewis, but the writing was already on the wall.

20. Swansea's second season in the Football League includes two new faces, Ernie Morley and Willie Davies, signed in exchange for a 10s 6d donation to Rhymney.

21. Swansea was the first Welsh club to play abroad in 1923. Twelve months later the club was invited back. This snapshot was taken in Copenhagen. Included in the group are Milne, Bellamy, Langford, Collins, Fowler, Thompson, Deacon, Morley and manager Joe Bradshaw.

22. Triple champions ... the Swansea team, captained by Joe Sykes (seated fourth from left, second row) which won the Third Division Championship in 1924-25 and lifted the Southern League and Welsh League titles. back row, from left: W Wishart, Whitehead, Lewis, Hole, McPherson, E Edwards (trainer), Collins, Bellamy, Morley, G Hart (groundsman); third row: J Bradshaw (manager), Rouse, Forbes, Hutchinson, Trench, Robson, Denoon, Davies, Handley, Morris, S B Williams; second row: T M Martin (director), D J Bassett (director), T Evans (director), Sykes, O Evans (chairman), Fowler, T M White, B W Jones (director), J B Owen. in front: Thomas, Langford, Corkindale, Deacon, Milne, Evans, Thompson, Humphries.

23. Jack Fowler wh scored five goals in the 6 win over Charlton durir the promotion season.

24. Joe Sykes who had such a great influence, first as a player, later discovering players like Ivor Allchurch and guiding their careers.

25. Defender Sam Langford, 79 League games 1923-27.

26. By 1927-28 the promotion side had started to break up but Sykes, McPherson, Hole, Deacon, Wilf Lewis, Milne and Collins were still in the picture.

The Great Depression

By the end of the 1929-30 season there were few players left from the original promotion side and the break-up of the team under Thompson signalled a period of depression which lasted until the start of the Second World War in 1939. Both Thompson and Neil Harris, his successor as manager, failed to arrest the slide and the club walked a tightrope in the Second Division at the end of several seasons.

In 1930 three points saved them from going down while in 1931, 1934 and 1938 only a win in the last game kept Swansea up. By the middle of the decade an appeal was launched with the prime objective of "Saving the club from decline" and the *Evening Post* played a significant part in the campaign by starting a "Shilling Fund".

A heavyweight boxing match, a dance and hundreds of smaller events also raised much needed cash, part of which Harris used to strengthen the team. But the club's fortunes remained at a low ebb and Swansea never finished higher than tenth during the thirties.

With the break-up of the original promotion side Thompson was forced to blood a number of new players. Among them was Ronnie Williams, a talented local boy who scored a hat-trick on his debut. Williams, a bustling centre forward, was popular with the fans and he rewarded their enthusiasm by emerging as top scorer in 1930 and sharing the distinction with Easton the following year.

Williams continued to shape up, together with Harry Hanford - another local youngster - and learned quickly from the more experienced members of the team.

At the end of the 1930-31 season, Hole and Deacon left, having played almost 700 games and having scored more than 120 goals between them. Now only Sykes remained of the old promotion side.

After the record-breaking achievements of the twenties, life at the club was tame by comparison until the arrival of Cyril Pearce from Newport at the beginning of the 1931-32 campaign. Pearce scored 35 goals that winter - a record which few players since have come close to breaking - but his stay was short. Swansea sold their goal scoring forward to Charlton and signed another Newport player, Tudor Martin, as his replacement. Martin started the 1932-33 season by scoring three goals in four games and was top scorer in three of the next four seasons.

Despite the presence of reliable centre half Hanford, goalkeeper Ferguson, the experienced Sykes, Sid Lawrence, a promising full back, and the return of Willie Davies, Swansea still failed to make much impression. The departure of the free scoring

27. Fed up with the standard team pose this *Daily Sketch* photographer in the 1930s tried a different line-up. Judging by the faces and the records it wasn't repeated too often.

Ronnie Williams to Newcastle did not help matters, but the move finally brought recognition from Wales which had been long overdue. Hanford eventually left as well, transferred to Sheffield Wednesday, but not before captaining Swansea to an FA Cup victory over First Division Stoke. The Potteries team included an exciting new discovery - Stanley Matthews.

At the same time as Matthews was starting out on a career which would bring him back to Vetch Field 30 years later, the long-serving Sykes was reaching the end of his. Two seasons later in 1937, he was followed into retirement by another stalwart, Wilf Milne.

Even though Harris continually rang the changes in an effort to recapture the success of the twenties, somehow the surgery never quite worked. Williams and Pearce returned to give the side that extra bit of experience up front but when Pearce was injured, Swansea turned to Len Emmanuel. The switch to centre forward paid off for a while but the departures continued: Jack Warner to Manchester United and George Lowrie to Preston.

Swansea's Silver Jubilee season, 1937-38, was disastrous. The club were beaten 8-1 by Fulham at Craven Cottage, their biggest defeat in the League, and in the last match of the season top scorer Harry Lewis scored the all-important goal which kept Swansea in the Second Division.

Throughout all the problems, a number of players remained loyal, none more so than Reuben Simons, a polished centre half whose No. 5 spot in the Swansea line-up would be taken over by his son-in-law Brian Purcell 30 years later in a memorable 1964 FA Cup run.

With the outbreak of war imminent, Swansea continued to struggle despite the arrival of big Bill Imrie from Newcastle for a club record £1,500 and Welsh international centre forward Tommy Bamford from Manchester United.

At the end of the 1938-39 season Harris left, but his successor Haydn Green and new chairman Abe Freedman would have to wait six years to get their plans for the future off the ground.

Unlike 1914 there was no question of football continuing once Hitler's armies threatened to engulf Europe. Conscription was introduced and the League programme was abandoned. Swansea kept going with friendlies and regional competition but had to move down the road to St. Helen's when Vetch Field was requisitioned for anti-aircraft purposes. That presented a problem because the St. Helen's lease prohibited professional sport being played on the hallowed turf. The obstacle was finally overcome when the rugby club surrendered the lease.

Swansea now began to recruit youngsters who were not old enough to be called up. The club finished its eighteen-match season bottom of six teams in the Football League West, but the experience proved invaluable for Roy Paul, Frankie Squires, Payne, Allen, Burns, Comley and Trevor Ford. Forces players had an opportunity, too, and that's how the club discovered Reg Weston who played such a key role in Swansea's promotion team in the immediate postwar years.

Among the guest players during that short League season were Leslie Jones, a Welsh international then with Arsenal, and Swansea-born Ernie Jones who was on Bolton's books. Both returned to join the Vetch Field staff after the war.

28. Harry Hanford, 200 League games 1927-36.

29. Cyril Pearce, a record 35 League goals in 1931-32.

11. In consideration of the observance by the said Player of the terms, provisions and conditions of this Agreement, the said _Jas H Thomson_ on behalf of the Club hereby agrees that the said Club shall pay to the said Player the sum of £3-0-0 per week from _7th October 1931_ to _____ and the sum of £_____ per week from _____ to _7th May 1932_ and in addition, the said Club agrees to pay the said Player the sum of £1-0-0 per week when the said Player is playing in any recognized First Eleven match.

12. In addition to the wages set forth in the next preceding clause, the said Player shall be paid all Bonuses on results of matches as notified by the Club and permitted to be paid by the Rules of the various Associations, Leagues, and Combinations of which the Club is a member.

13. If at any time during the period of this Agreement the wages herein agreed to be paid shall be in excess of the wages permitted to be paid by the Club to the Player in accordance with the Rules of the Football League, the wages to be paid to the Player shall be the amount the Club is entitled to pay by League Rules in force from time to time, and this Agreement shall be read and construed as if it were varied accordingly.

14. This Agreement shall cease and determine on _7th May 1932_ unless the same shall have been previously determined in accordance with the provisions hereinbefore set forth.

As Witness the hands of the said parties the day and year first aforesaid.

Signed by the said _Jas H Thomson_

and _R. R. Simons_

in the presence of _____

(Signature) _____

(Occupation) _____

(Address) _____

Jas H Thomson,

Reuben Rhys Simons

FORM OF NOTICE TO TERMINATE AGREEMENT.

I, the undersigned, as Manager for and on behalf of the Swansea Town Association Football Club Limited, do hereby give you _____ days' notice of the intention of the said Club to terminate the Agreement of service dated the _____ day of _____ 19 _____ entered into between you and the Club on the following grounds.

And further take notice that you have a right to appeal to the Management Committee of the Football League, but such appeal must be made within seven days of the receipt of this Notice. Such appeal will be heard within ten days of the receipt of the notice of appeal from you. If dissatisfied with the decision of the Management Committee you have a further right of appeal to the Appeals Committee of the Football League appointed for that purpose by the Football Association, but such further appeal must be made by you within seven days of the receipt of the intimation of the decision of the Management Committee and must be accompanied by a deposit of £5. The Appeals Committee will hear such appeal within ten days of the receipt of the notice of appeal.

30. A typical players' contract for the 1931-32 season - £3 basic with an extra £1 for any first team match.

31. H A Anstiss, six goals in 29 League games 1931-33.

32. H J Boston, 18 League games 1931-32.

33. Walter Bussey, 18 League goals in 74 matches 1934-37.

34. Centre of attention, not the players this time but the gentleman in the flat cap who clearly has something to divulge about the state of play that he does not want his cigar smoking friend to hear. Joe Sykes captained this team.

35. Special training at Langland Bay, and Jack Pears is about to get a ducking from Tommy Olsen, Stan Moore, Reuben Simons, Joe Brain and Tommy Foster.

36. Back on dry land the training method changes as demonstrated by Dakins and Lowrie, D J Lewis and Caldwell, Milne and Walton, Simons and Warner.

37. Joe Brain, 25 goals in 51 League
games 1934-37.

38. Peter Leyland, 29 League games
1935-39.

39. George Lowrie, 19 League
games 1936-38.

41. *above:* Cyril Greene, two goals in 12 League
games 1936-38.

40. *left:* Reuben Simons looking for a little
divine guidance.

42. There was no shortage of optimism in the thirties despite little success.

43-45. *left:* Wilf Milne played all but one of his club record 585 League appearances as a full-back. But at Leicester on 27 March 1937 he was pressed into service as emergency goalkeeper when Stan Moore was taken ill and HE kept the Leicester attack at bay to earn Swansea a point from a goalless draw. *centre:* Tommy Bamford, 14 goals in 36 League games 1938-39 after his transfer from Manchester United. *right:* Bill Imrie, 27 League games 1938-39. A Scot from Methill, Fife, Imrie played for St Johnstone, Blackburn Rovers and Newcastle United before joining Swansea in July 1938.

46. This mid thirties line-up includes Syd Lawrence, Peter Leyland, Tom Emmanuel, Jack Warner, Idris Lewis, Ronnie Williams, Walter Bussey and Tommy Caldwell.

Rationing and Riches

Most people look upon the immediate postwar period as the boom years - and they were probably not far wrong. Ten thousand turned up at Vetch Field just for a trial match, and 20,000 for a League game was considered quite normal.

It was a time when rival supporters could swap jokes instead of punches on the terraces and still leave the ground without clutching each others throats whatever the result. Football provided the perfect antidote to remove some of the pain of the previous six years and Swansea's supporters had a lot to be thankful for. The Swansea production line read like a who's who of the game: Charles, Allchurch, Medwin, Jones, Ford, Paul, Weston, Burns, Griffiths, Kiley - the list was endless.

Vetch Field provided a rich vein of talent for the bigger clubs, and one by one all the top names left, but not before Swansea audiences had been thrilled. One of the first to go was Ford, a PT instructor in the Army who returned for the 1945-46 season as Swansea mustered their troops for the start of the League season twelve months later. They included the romantically named Kitchener "Kit" Fisher, a full back, and seven-goal Joe Payne, nicknamed for his goal scoring exploits in one match with Northampton.

Ford, a small but powerful centre forward, scored 40 goals during that transitional period which would have created a club record had the League restarted. The fearless Ford quickly attracted the top clubs and it came as little surprise to Swansea fans when he was transferred to Aston Villa for £10,000 halfway through the 1946-47 season. The money could not make up for the material shortages which rationing brought, but manager Green's public appeal for soap and clothing coupons ensured that the team was always well turned out.

Green, always prepared to look beyond the problems of the day, gave the go-ahead for the installation of a broadcasting system at the ground, after being appointed secretary on the retirement of S B Williams who had filled the post since the club was founded.

At the same time as manager-secretary Green was pressing ahead with his team strengthening, Swansea schoolboys, who were regularly attracting 20,000 even before the war, were providing the first link in the production line. John Charles, Terry Medwin and Glyn Davies were among the first to join that long chain which would lead beyond Vetch Field.

Of the three, Charles was the only one who never played a League game for the club. He was on the Vetch Field staff as a 16 year old, and even played in the Football Combination. However, because he was an amateur, Leeds spirited him away right under Swansea's nose and signed him as a professional. It was all perfectly legal and above

47. The team which clinched the Third Division South title. *back row, left to right:* Sam McGrory, Edgar Newall, Terry Elwell, Danny Canning, Jack Parry, Stan Richards, Jim Feeney, Rory Keane. *seated:* Billy McCandless, manager, Billy Lucas, Roy Paul, Frank Burns, Reg Weston, Jack O'Driscoll, Frank Scrine, Joe Payne, Frank Barson, trainer.

board, but the rules governing young players were changed shortly after as a result of the Charles case - little consolation for Swansea. The pioneering trio were all still too young to help Green who quickly realised that the team he had assembled was not strong enough to sustain a challenge when the Football League restarted in 1946-47.

Green turned across the Irish Sea for fresh talent and brought back Norman Lockhart and Sam McGrory from his first scouting trip. Both players scored on their debut with McGrory going on to hit 46 in 103 League games. The Celtic connection was further strengthened when Jim Feeney joined the staff. Feeney, a polished full back, quickly became a firm favourite with the crowd. While Feeney was making his debut, a young player was starting out on a distinguished career, in the club's Welsh League side. His name was Ivor Allchurch.

Despite the growing Irish influence, Swansea lost their Second Division status and were relegated along with Newport. By then Swansea had sold winger Ernie Jones to Tottenham for £7,000 and the only crumb of comfort for the hard working Green was the success of the club's reserve side who were the first winners of the Football Combination Cup.

With Joe Sykes back at the club to assist trainer Frank Barson, a former England centre half with a fearless reputation, Green boldly pursued the Irish policy. Prior to the start of the club's first season in the Third Division South since 1924-25, Green recruited talented winger Jack O'Driscoll from Cork for £3,000 and Rory Keane. He also paid £3,000 to Newport for Frank Rawcliffe, but the newcomers failed to arrest the slide.

After a disappointing start to the new season, Green's time at the club was clearly running out. But he made one last unsuccessful attempt to bring in a big name player by putting in a bid for Tommy Lawton. Ten days later he resigned.

His successor Billy McCandless was already something of a legend in South Wales having guided both Cardiff and Newport back to the Second Division. Within eighteen months of his arrival that was to become a hat-trick. McCandless inherited the nucleus of a powerful side. Six weeks before he took over, Swansea whipped Leyton Orient 5-0 with a side comprising goalkeeper Jack Parry, Feeney, Keane, Paul, Weston, Burns, O'Driscoll, McGrory, James, Squires and Lockhart. By the time McCandless arrived, Lockhart had been transferred to Coventry and Squires to Plymouth. Swansea had a ready replacement for Lockhart in the shape of Frank Scrine, but the money enabled McCandless to make his most significant capture, paying Swindon a club record of £11,000 for Billy Lucas.

Swansea finished the season strongly in fifth spot, McGrory was top scorer with sixteen and Lucas was making his presence felt - the prospects looked good. Those hopes were well founded, and the arrival of Stan Richards from Cardiff merely confirmed the optimism. Richards scored 26 goals in 32 games during that first season and the support from McGrory (19) and Scrine (18) underlined the scoring ability of the new-look forward line.

With Lucas very much the general of the side and Weston solid and reliable in defence, Swansea raced to the Third Division South Championship and set several records into the bargain including seventeen successive wins at home and the best goal difference (+53) which still stands today.

McCandless had made his mark and clearly felt the team did not need too much strengthening. Brothers Cyril and Gilbert Beech arrived from Merthyr and made 290 League appearances between them. Cyril, a winger with pace, was nicknamed Tulyar after the famous racehorse, and the wags at the Richardson Street end of the ground frequently claimed that if they opened the gates he would run straight through them. Shortly after the arrival of Cyril and his brother, who operated at left back, Dai Thomas made his debut at inside forward, the start of a long career which spanned eleven years and almost 300 League matches.

The comings and goings continued despite the insistence from chairman Abe Freedman that the club was not going to sell players and spend extravagently on new ones. Feeney and McGrory were transferred to Ipswich, Paul went to Manchester City for £18,000 following the famous Bogata incident when he flew to South America to sign for a local club only to return within two weeks. Paul was considered one of the finest half backs in the country - as Maine Road fans were to discover - but Swansea, despite mourning his departure, had to look ahead.

There was a new generation coming though the club ranks. Not least among them was Ivor Allchurch, a tall, blond inside left who made his debut at Christmas 1949 and was quickly dubbed the golden boy of Welsh football. There were two other debutants that season - Tom Kiley, a tall, commanding centre half who deputised for Weston, and Harry Griffiths, a winger home on leave from the Army. Swansea also signed schoolboy John King, but with Danny Canning in goal, the teenage prospect had to wait twelve months to make his debut as an amateur. It was the start of a lengthy career spanning fourteen years and a record 368 appearances for a Swansea goalkeeper.

Swansea finished a respectable eighth in their first season back in the Second Division, but there was just as much interest in the performance of the town's schoolboy team who lifted the English Trophy for the second time since the war. The side was captained by the diminutive Cliff Jones and his pedigree - he was the son of former Swansea player Ivor Jones - marked him down as a prospect for the future. The team also included Mel Charles.

One of the other major problems since returning to the Second Division was the lack of a goal scorer which was only resolved when Swansea agreed to pay Manchester City £7,500 for centre forward Ronnie Turnbull. He scored eight goals in 12 matches, which helped to avoid relegation, and in 1951-52, another largely unsuccessful season, he top scored with 20.

Within the space of twelve months, Swansea were blooding more youngsters, including wingers

Terry Medwin and Len Allchurch, Ivor's younger brother. McCandless also introduced Davo Williams, a sturdy wing half. At the start of the 1951-52 season, when admission prices were increased to 1s 6d and the maximum wage was raised to £14, Swansea signed winger Alf Bellis from Bury..

The club continued to struggle in the League, almost went down and lost Ivor Allchurch as well when Swansea's bankers ordered the club to reduce its debt. Swansea finished 19th after winning the last match at Rotherham but the need to sell Allchurch was removed when three new directors joined the board. They included Philip Holden who took over as chairman and later became president. That season also marked the end of an era. Chairman Abe Freedman, the driving force before and after the war, resigned because of ill-health and was made a life member to honour his many years of devoted service to the club. With the Allchurch threat safely removed, Swansea looked ahead with optimism, but the break-up of the promotion side continued: Burns joined Southend; O'Driscoll left for Llanelli; and Weston moved to Derby.

Swansea kept faith with a policy to develop local talent and the club's debts of £20,000 meant that McCandless was forced to blood some of his youngsters a little sooner than he had anticipated. Among them were two 17 year olds, Cliff Jones and Mel Charles, and before the end of the 1952-53 season, Mel marked brother John, centre forward with Leeds, in a memorable Vetch Field match which Swansea won 3-2. Two goals were scored by Terry Medwin, who was top scorer that season, and the third came from Cliff Jones.

By then Cliff's brother Bryn had joined the club

after completing his National Service and Swansea had four sets of brothers on the staff. Apart from the Jones boys, there were Ivor and Len Allchurch, Cyril and Gilbert Beech and Alan and Colin Hole, sons of former player Billy Hole.

Swansea played their first match under floodlights at Cheltenham, (an unlikely venue, but things were still rather gloomy on the Vetch Field front where the reluctant McCandless was repeatedly asked to take a more active part in training.

Despite the board's growing concern, Swansea continued to unearth top schoolboy prospects. The town team again beat Chesterfield to lift the English Trophy and the outstanding player was Mel Nurse. McCandless, meanwhile, had warned about the need for careful control in the handling of so many young charges and the poor results at the start of the 1953-54 season underlined his thinking. His problems were not helped when Swansea sold Frank Scrine to Plymouth and allowed Billy Lucas to become Newport's player-manager, but the retirement of Barson through ill-health meant that he had to take greater involvement on the training field.

Results, however, did not improve, despite the fact that McCandless was able to field so many talented players. At one stage, they were all Welshmen - King, Charles, Thomas, Hole (A), Kiley, Williams, Allchurch (L), Jones (B), Medwin, Allchurch (I), Jones (C).

The turning point came in June 1954 when Swansea appointed Ronnie Burgess, released by Tottenham, as player-coach. It was an inspired choice and together with Kiley and Charles the trio

48. No problems filling the ground, not even for a trial match. More than 15,000 turned up at Vetch Field for the traditional pipe opener in 1951. Reg Weston and Billy Morris are in pursuit of the ball.

formed an impressive half back line which helped to haul Swansea up from 20th to 10th place with Ivor Allchurch top scorer for the second successive season.

The arrival of Arthur Willis, then 34 but still a stylish full back, for a modest £3,000, proved another shrewd investment, but it was the goal scoring exploits of the forward line, average age 23 which helped to keep the terraces packed to capacity. Ivor Allchurch, 20 goals, Harry Griffiths, 16, Terry Medwin, 12, and Cliff Jones, 10, illustrated the point, while Mel Charles chipped in with 13 as well.

The influence of Joe Sykes, now chief trainer, was reflected when two of his young proteges, Mel Charles and Cliff Jones, made a presentation to their mentor with a message which said what so many others felt: "In appreciation of the great help which you have given us."

Sykes played an even more influential role in the 1955-56 season following the death of McCandless who led a side he largely inherited back into the Second Division and introduced so many talented young players through the Swansea ranks. Burgess took over as team manager, established a three-man selection committee with Sykes and Ivor Allchurch, and after a shaky start, Swansea led the Second

Division table going into November.

Just as Swansea's faithful followers were beginning to savour the prospect of First Division football, tragedy struck when centre half Tom Kiley suffered a serious knee injury in training. Swansea were thrashed 6-1 in their next match, a top-of-the-table game against Leicester. The club had no ready-made replacement and although they tried half a dozen candidates no-one measured up to Kiley's influence.

Mel Charles, Steve Leavy, Jim Pressdee, better known for his exploits as a Glamorgan cricketer, Dudley Peake, 17 year old Mel Nurse, and even Burgess himself were pressed into service while Tom Brown, originally signed from Doncaster to plug the gap, played just once that season at right back in the final game.

Even though Swansea were still in a challenging position at Easter they missed out, finishing tenth. They then sold top scorer Medwin to Tottenham for £18,000, which marked the start of another exodus that ripped the heart out of the side which had come so near to fulfilling a long cherished dream.

Swansea bought three players with part of the money they received from the Medwin deal but the insistence on operating at the lower end of the transfer market continued to prove disastrous.

49. Another view of the packed North Bank, now completely covered, as Terry Medwin challenges the Fulham goalkeeper with Harry Griffiths on hand to support. No need for fencing or segregation in those days.

Derek King, Mal Morris and Derek Blackburn cost a total of £3,000. King signed without a medical from Cardiff and was forced to quit after five games because of a knee injury. Blackburn and Morris both failed to establish themselves. The problems mounted when Kiley was forced to give up his fight for fitness following a knee operation which was quickly followed by transfer requests from Ivor Allchurch, Cliff Jones and Des Palmer who still finished the season top scorer with 21 goals.

Allchurch was still the shining light, playing brilliantly in a largely unsuccessful side, including a scoring turn of nine consecutive games - a record which still stands today.

Despite the absence of any new signings Swansea were still drawing crowds of 25,000 plus at the start of the 1957-58 campaign, even though a centre stand season ticket cost £16 16s.

Swansea supporters, not for the first time, had cause to question whether the board really had First Division ambitions given their recent track record and it wasn't until Cliff Jones was sold to Tottenham for a new British record of £35,000 that Burgess was allowed to move a little higher in the quality of incoming players. Pat Terry arrived from Newport for £5,000, Ipswich winger Billy Reed cost £3,000 and Swansea eventually succeeded in signing former Arsenal centre half Ray Daniel for a similar fee.

Swansea finished the season strongly but it was only a 2-1 win over Bristol City at Ashton Gate on the last day of the season which kept Burgess and his players in the Second Division. For a Swansea team which had supplied five players - Cliff Jones, Dai Thomas, Mel Charles, Len Allchurch and hat-trick hero Des Palmer - to the Wales side which whipped East Germany 4-1, it was a close run thing; far too close as Burgess was to discover after Trevor Morris had been appointed general manager. Within a month Burgess, who had come so close to steering the club into the First Division, had resigned and a new era was born.

Among his last transactions was the sale of Bryn Jones and Dudley Peake to Newport for £5,000, money that was used to buy Norman Lawson from Bury and Wendell Morgan from Gillingham.

Swansea, with Barrie Jones and Mike Johnson on amateur forms, blooded 17 year old Herbie Williams just two months into the 1958-59 season and were evidently impressed by his performance in a 5-0 win over Sunderland. Ivor Allchurch scored four of the goals, his last major contribution before joining Newcastle in a £25,000 deal which brought Reg Davies to Swansea. Morris bought Colin Webster with part of the money and the former Manchester United forward proved a bargain at £6,000, scoring 67 goals in 159 League appearances.

Morris continued to wheel and deal in an effort to improve the fortunes of the club and for several seasons the policy worked. His bargain hunting was usually successful. Graham Williams arrived from Everton for £5,000 and quickly earned the nickname Flicka to underline his darting runs down the wing. Des Palmer moved to Liverpool in exchange for £4,000 and Roy Saunders, a wing half who

developed a close relationship with Harry Griffiths. Before the end of the 1958-59 season the club lost another of its favourite sons, Mel Charles, who was transferred to Arsenal for a club record £40,000 with Peter Davies travelling in the other direction from Highbury.

Morris still had not finished his rebuilding. By the start of the 1959-60 season Brayley Reynolds arrived from Cardiff for a four figure fee and went on to score 57 goals in 151 League appearances. David Dodson joined the club from Arsenal for a small fee, Dixie Hale was offered a job following a successful trial and Everton full back Alan Sanders signed in a £6,000 deal.

With Mel Nurse outstanding in the heart of the defence and two more youngsters, Barrie Jones and Brian Purcell starting out on their careers, the prospects looked good as Swansea's world renowned Mumbles train was making its last journey.

50. Legendary trainer Frank Barson. Tough and direct he frequently told players: "If it moves kick it, if it does not, kick it until it does."

51. It's Boxing Day 1949 at Builth Wells where Swansea's A team, average age 17, played a local team to celebrate the opening of a new ground. Three of the players became senior Welsh internationals, another found fame as a Glamorgan cricketer. *standing, from left to right:* Les Simpson, Derek Michaels, Johnny King, Jim Pressdee, unknown, Brian Sykes. *seated:* Len Allchurch, Roy Jones, Roger Howells, Des Palmer, Colin Hole.

52-54. *left:* Manager Haydn Green led the postwar revival. *centre:* 7-goal Joe Payne, 53 League appearances 1946-49. *right:* Roy Paul, a native of the Rhonddha, joined Manchester City from Swansea in July 1950, for £25,000. He captained Manchester City's FA Cup winning side of 1956 before joining Worcester in June 1957 as player-manager. At one time Paul also considered playing football in Colombia for Bogota but elected to stay in Britain.

55. Reg Weston, who led Swansea back to the Second Division.

56. Arthur Willis, ageing but influential.

57-8. The Irish connection ... Jack O'Driscoll and Rory Keane.

59. Billy Lucas, the general of the promotion side.

60. Frank Squires, a war-time international who played in the immediate postwar years.

61. Cliff Jones heading for the top.

2. Trevor Ford, first of the major postwar transfers.

63. Ronnie Turnbull, 35 goals in 67 League matches 1950-55.

64. Steve Leavy, 36 League games 1950-58.

65. Johnny King, a goalkeeping record - 368 League games 1950-64.

66. Ivor Allchurch, regarded by many as the greatest inside-forward of his day.

67. Bryn Jones, joined brother Cliff after National Service.

68. Gilbert Beech, 157 League appearances 1949-58.

69. Dai Thomas, 298 League games 1949-60.

70. Tom Kiley, a commanding centre-half. Barson once told him: "With a physique like yours you should have a cemetery of centre-forwards".

71. Left back Rory Keane punches the ball over the bar after goalkeeper Jack Parry had been beaten in this 1950 FA Cup tie against Arsenal at Highbury. Wales international Wally Barnes converted the spot kick.

72. Arsenal goalkeeper George Swindin dives at the feet of Swansea centre-forward Frank Scrine.

73. Goalkeeper Johnny King saves at the feet of England international Tommy Lawton who was making his debut for Brentford in this 1952 Second Division match.

74. Swansea centre-half Reg Weston clears his lines under pressure from Tommy Lawton.

75. Ivor Allchurch and Ray Daniel congratulate each other after being called up by Wales. Looking on are Jack Parry, Gilbert Beech, Tom Kiley and Terry Elwell.

76. Even goalkeeper Johnny King has something in common with Harry Griffiths, Terry Medwin and Des Palmer. The trio all played centre forward at one time and King was pressed into emergency service up front during a Second Division match at Rotherham in 1956.

77. Mel Charles, 69 goals in 233 League games 1952-59.

78. Mel Nurse, debut at 17.

79. Listening attentively as Joe Sykes explains a point are Harry Griffiths, Gilbert Beech and Johnny King.

80. Tied up in knots ... Joe Sykes hands out the rope markers and skipping ropes as pre-season training gets under way.

81. Seven members of this mid 1950s line-up came through the Swansea schoolboy ranks. *standing, from left to right:* Arthur Willis, Tom Kiley, Johnny King, Ronnie Burgess, Dai Thomas, Mel Charles. *seated:* Len Allchurch, Harry Griffiths, Ivor Allchurch, Terry Medwin, Cliff Jones.

82. Davo Williams, 130 League appearances 1950-55.

83. Pat Terry, nine goals in 17 League games 1957-59.

45 Minutes from Wembley

Ask anyone what the Swinging Sixties meant to them, and the chances are the answers would range from the Beatles to England winning the World Cup.

Ask any Swans supporter and there's little doubt what the response would be - that memorable FA Cup march which swept the club into the semi-finals for the second time in their history.

In a decade when Swansea was created a city, became the first Welsh club to play in Europe and dropped from the Second Division to the Fourth in three seasons, that Cup run and the drama which accompanied it remains one of the great talking points even today.

That 1963-64 season started badly. Despite the arrival of Jimmy McLaughlin for a record £16,000 fee from Shrewsbury, and the promise of Welsh League recruits Brian Evans and John Roberts, any prospects of a Cup run seemed as remote as winning the Second Division Championship.

True to form, Swansea got it right for the Cup, overcoming Barrow 4-1 in the third round far more easily than most expected. On the day when Mike Johnson captained the team for the first time, Swansea romped home with goals from Brian Evans, Herbie Williams, Roy Evans and Eddie Thomas, signed the previous season from Blackburn.

Swansea went to Bramall Lane to face Sheffield United in the next round. They were very much the underdogs and it needed another Thomas goal to force a replay against a side which included former Vetch Field favourite Len Allchurch, sold three years earlier but destined to end his days on the ground where he and elder brother Ivor started their distinguished careers.

Suddenly cup fever gripped a club where gates had dropped to around 7,000 for League games. More than 24,000 watched the replay as Swansea produced a thrilling exhibition, winning 4-0 with goals from Thomas, McLaughlin and two from 20 year old inside forward Derek Draper.

Swansea took almost 9,000 fans to Stoke in the next round and earned a draw, despite an early goal from the legendary Stanley Matthews - his last goal in competitive matches. Incredibly he was 49 and had scored in a Cup tie between the clubs almost 30 years earlier.

Swansea's hero that day was two-goal Keith Todd, a short, stocky player who led the attack superbly after being restored to the Cup side. Todd was on target again in the replay, together with McLaughlin, as the Swans won 2-0 to set up a quarter-final meeting against mighty Liverpool at Anfield.

In eight visits to Merseyside Swansea had never won, and against a side containing household names like St. John, Yeats, Callaghan and Hunt, no one really expected an upset. Two Irishmen, McLaughlin and Noel Dwyer, ignored such pessimistic statistics and wrote their own names into the Swansea legend.

The gifted McLaughlin scored the first goal and then helped to set up a second for Thomas four minutes later. The rest of the match belonged to goalkeeper Dwyer who produced a series of breathtaking saves which many believe contributed to Ronnie Moran's penalty miss near the end. Swansea held on to win 2-1 which left Liverpool manager Bill Shankly adamant his side should have scored 14. Needless to say, Dwyer disagreed.

Having already beaten semi-final opponents Preston 5-1 at home and drawn at Deepdale, Swansea and their army of 30,000 fans, were quietly confident of success. But the clinging mud of Villa Park, a controversial penalty and a freak goal, sent Swansea sliding to a 2-1 defeat. Despite leading at the interval through McLaughlin, Swansea were rocked back on their heels when Dawson equalised from a penalty before Singleton drove in a speculative 40 yard shot which caught Dwyer, hero of the last round, completely by surprise. The disappointment was cushioned by a £17,000 profit from the Cup run but after three seasons of struggle in the Second Division changes were inevitable.

Change never worried manager Trevor Morris. From the day he arrived at the club in 1958 to the day he left in 1965, he established quite a reputation as a wheeler dealer in the transfer market. Among the arrivals at the start of the decade were Noel Dwyer, bought from West Ham for £3,500 and a Hungarian trialist John Haasz who never made the grade as a goalkeeper.

The changes came thick and fast at the start of the 1960-61 season. Floodlighting was installed at Vetch Field and Swansea teenager Keith Todd scored on his debut against Derby, as well as having a hand in the other goal scored by Len Allchurch in a 2-1 win. Before the end of the season Allchurch was transferred to Sheffield United for £14,000, signed by John Harris, a former Swansea player. The move did not go down well with supporters but Swansea, who turned down a £30,000 offer from Manchester United for Mel Nurse, insisted they had to balance the books which showed a £23,000 loss the previous season.

Nurse, anxious to play in the First Division, had his fourth transfer request turned down after Swansea had climbed to Second Division safety with an unbeaten run of 16 games which stretched to a record 19 at the start of the 1961-62 season.

By then inside forward Ken Morgans, a survivor of the Munich air disaster which claimed the lives of so many Busby Babes, had joined the club for £3,000 from Manchester United, and the Welsh Cup again resided in the Vetch Field boardroom.

Winning the magnificent trophy for the fourth time by beating Bangor in the final sent Swansea into the Cup-Winners' Cup - the first Welsh club to play in Europe.

The euphoria quickly evaporated, however, when Swansea came out of the hat alongside Motor Jena and found that they had to play the "home" leg against the crack East German team just across the German border in the Austrian town of Linz due to restrictions on movement throughout the Allied corridor in Berlin.

Despite drawing the first leg in Austria with goals from Brayley Reynolds and Mel Nurse, it was an ill fated trip The effects of all the travelling finally took a heavy toll when the team played the return game two days later without Colin Webster who had been sent off in Linz. Swansea crashed 5-1 in Jena and never found European competition to their liking even when they returned as Welsh Cup winners in the 1966-67 season. This time they lost 5-1 on aggregate to Slavia Sofia with a side ill equipped for such a demanding task.

Morris, armed with a new three year contract after that first European adventure and a £63,000 profit on transfer dealings, continued to ring the changes. He bought Peter Donnelly from Cardiff for £5,000 and sold him to Brighton six months later for £1,000 more. David Dodson went to Portsmouth for £4,000 and by the start of the 1962-63 season Eddie Thomas had arrived from Blackburn, Swansea having spent the £10,000 received for Donnelly and Reg Davies who joined Carlisle. It did not end there. Nurse finally got his wish and joined Middlesbrough for £25,000, a transfer which prompted a hostile reaction from supporters claiming that Morris was nothing more than a business manager. To an extent they were right but Swansea, having reported a loss of £7,000 to their shareholders, insisted that they had to balance the books and the sale of Alan Sanders to Brighton for £5,500 was predictable.

After three successive seasons in the lower regions of the Second Division and only the Cup run to cushion the disappointment, the Morris style of change continued. Three stalwarts, Harry Griffiths, Johnny King and Graham Williams moved out, Griffiths into non-League management at Merthyr after 424 League appearances including a memorable game when he outplayed the legendary Stanley Matthews from his favourite left back slot. King, a Vetch fixture for 15 seasons, made 368 appearances, a club record for a goalkeeper.

84. One step from Wembley. Swansea's semi-final squad for the FA Cup tie against Preston. *back row, from left to right:* Walter Robbins, trainer, Roy Evans, Peter Davies, Noel Dwyer, Brian Hughes, Herbie Williams, Brian Purcell, Trevor Morris, manager. *seated:* Brayley Reynolds, Barrie Jones, Keith Todd, Mike Johnson, Derek Draper, Eddie Thomas, Brian Evans, Jimmy McLaughlin.

Swansea turned to Manchester United and Ronnie Briggs for King's replacement which meant that Dwyer, hero in that memorable Cup tie at Liverpool, was no longer regarded as No. 1. By mid-season, with another loss reported to shareholders, Dwyer was transferred to Plymouth for £7,500 - £4,000 more than Morris paid for him when he signed him five seasons earlier.

By then the side which was lacking in confidence had been stripped of the experienced Eddie Thomas, a £6,000 Derby signing, and Welsh international winger Barrie Jones for whom Plymouth paid £45,000. The replacements came thick and fast: Albert Harley from Shrewsbury; George Kirby from Coventry; John McGuigan from Southampton; and Willie Humphries, one of the smallest wingers in the game, from Coventry. It was nothing more than a holding operation, but this time the Morris magic did not work. Swansea were relegated to the Third Division and it would be another 14 years before the club regained its Second Division status, led by a man who at the time was a 16 year old playing on a Cardiff park.

Inevitably Morris resigned having negotiated a £25,000 pay-off and the club turned to one of its former players, Glyn Davies, who took over as the first Swansea-bred manager at the start of the 1965-66 season. He immediately brought Ivor Allchurch back from Cardiff and signed goalkeeper George Heyes from Leicester.

Prior to Davies' return, Swansea had introduced two players who would find fame elsewhere: John Roberts, and Giorgio Chinaglia who was given a free transfer and then went on to make his name and his fortune in America and Italy.

Despite all the departures, Swansea were still signing talented young players such as 16 year old goalkeeper Dai Davies from Ammanford and 17 year old Swansea schools product Geoff Thomas. But manager Davies quickly realised that it would take more than the experience and knowledge of the stylish Allchurch to stop the rot. At the start of the 1966-67 season he turned to Vic Gomersall, a full back with Manchester City, and Dennis Coughlin, an inside forward at Bournemouth.

By the end of October, Swansea had gained just five points from the opening nine games and Davies' contract was terminated. This time Swansea turned to 68 year old Joe Sykes as caretaker with Walter Robbins as his right hand man.

The more permanent position was filled in February 1967 when Billy Lucas, one of the toughest tackling half backs of his day, returned to the club as manager to work closely with Sykes and Allchurch, the senior professional.

Lucas moved swiftly to sign Joe Davis from Bristol Rovers and goalkeeper Dilwyn John from Cardiff, but the double signing came too late to prevent Swansea slipping into the Fourth Division for the first time in their history.

Still, Lucas had the nucleus of a useful team, to which he added John Bird from Newport, David Lawrence, son of the prewar club captain, and Billy

85. All the best. Swansea captain Mike Johnson greets Preston skipper Nobby Lawton before the 1964 semi-final.

86. Preston goalkeeper Alan Kelly clears the danger under pressure from Eddie Thomas during the FA Cup semi-final against Preston.

Screen whose younger brother Tony also played for the club around the same time.

Swansea, however, were still losing heavily - £500 per week - so player of the year John Roberts was sold to Northampton to placate the bank. There was another departure, too. At 38 Ivor Allchurch had reached the end of a distinguished career. Sykes had discovered the fair haired genius on a local park at 14. Having taken the place of a boy who had not turned up, the promise was evident then, even though he was playing in long trousers and ordinary shoes. Later he swapped them for the real thing, won 68 Welsh caps, a record he held for many years, played almost 700 League games and scored 251 goals. Few players in the Allchurch hey-day of the fifties and sixties possessed his vision and goal scoring instinct. Even today, most regard him as the greatest inside forward of his generation.

The only bright spot from that 1967-68 season was the FA Cup run which brought Arsenal to Vetch Field, but there was a scare on the morning of the game when groundsman Sid Tucker discovered that vandals had sawn through the goalposts at the town end. After some hasty repairs the Cup tie went ahead. Bobby Gould scored the only goal of the match for the Gunners in front of a record 32,786 gate which produced receipts of £9,475.

Two days later Swansea were knocked out of the Welsh Cup by Newport and they won only one of the next nine matches before a serious fire damaged the grandstand and destroyed the treatment room.

By the start of the following season Mel Nurse had rejoined the club, Lucas paid £5,000 to Walsall for Jimmy McMorran and after the departure of the long-serving Sykes, Robbins became assistant manager with Harry Griffiths returning as chief trainer. But all the pre-season optimism at the start of the 1968-69 campaign quickly evaporated with a string of poor results to which Lucas responded by recruiting Alan Williams to stiffen the defence and Alfie Biggs to stimulate the attack.

In January Brian Hughes left to join Atlanta Chiefs, just before two of his contemporaries, Roy Evans and Brian Purcell, by now playing for Hereford, were tragically killed in a car crash.

Lucas, keen to recruit young blood, handed opportunities to Doug Rosser, Wayne Williams, Carl Slee, Clive Slattery and Terry Cotton, but after a heartening end of season win over Lincoln he suddenly resigned to go back into business in Newport.

Despite selling players at regular intervals to make ends meet, much to the annoyance of the vociferous Ginger Group during the sixties, Swansea were in debt to the tune of £48,000 and, on top of that burden, they had to find a new manager to spark a change in fortunes.

The shake up came in the shape of a consortium of local businessmen, headed by the persistent Malcolm Struel, who was a member of the Ginger Group. The newly created board of directors included newcomers Terry Francis, David Goldstone, Richard Englert, Ivor Pursey and Derek Wignall. Only two members of the old board remained, Trevor Wood and Peter Walters.

Struel, in particular, had been highly critical of the policy of selling so many players. He was determined to change it, but little did he know then how long it was going to take to achieve that and bring success back to the club.

87. Jimmy McLaughlin ploughs his way through the Villa Park mud to put Swansea ahead in the semi-final before turning away in jubilant mood.

88. Swansea 1 Preston 0. Jimmy McLaughlin celebrates.

89. Goalkeeper Noel Dwyer is beaten by Alex Dawson's penalty equaliser for Preston in the semi-final.

90. Dwyer was very much the hero of the quarter-final round against Liverpool at Anfield. Here he makes a critical save watched by grateful Swansea team mates Johnson, Hughes and Williams.

91. Dwyer saves the day yet again.

92. Dwyer's defences were pierced just once by Peter Thompson's shot which Brian Purcell tries in vain to keep out.

93. Ronnie Moran's critical penalty miss for Liverpool as Dwyer dives to his right.

94. My hero. A Swansea supporter congratulates Dwyer
after the Anfield triumph.

95. Dwyer mobbed as he leaves the field at Anfield complete with 3s 9d picked up in the Swansea goalmouth from the generous Kop fans.

96. Jimmy McLaughlin (*left*) and Brian Hughes offer their own thanks after Dwyer's memorable performance.

97. Right, who've we got next? Players and staff listen to the Cup draw with Harry Griffiths (*sixth from left*) seeking help for a favourable tie.

98. Wishing for success. Swansea's players off on another Cup journey.

99. Eddie Thomas, 23 goals in 68 League games 1962-65.

100. Colin Webster, 67 goals in 159 League appearances 1958-63.

01. Roy Evans, tragically killed in a car crash 1968.

102. Reg Davies, 29 goals in 108 League games 1958-62.

103. Georgio Chinaglia, who played in America after being released.

104-107. *left:* That winning feeling. Captain Brian Hughes holds up the Welsh Cup after the club's 1966 triumph, watched by Denise Paton, Swansea's mascot in Welsh costume during their Cup exploits. *below:* Arsenal forward Bobby Gould knocks Swansea out of the FA Cup with this 1968 match-winner in front of a record Vetch Field crowd. *above left:* Herbie Williams, 102 goals in 515 League games. *above right:* Graham 'Flicka' Williams, 20 goals in 89 League matches 1958-62.

108-110. *left:* Hard at it. Brian Evans and Herbie Williams put in some punishing pre-season training. *above and below:* Ivor Allchurch, just as lethal off the tee and on the greens as he was on the pitch. Among the admirers are Brian Hughes, Roy Evans, Herbie Williams Jimmy McLaughlin and Geoff Thomas.

111. Playing on towards the end of the 1967-68 season with the fire damaged stand in the background.

112. John Charles drops in at Vetch Field for a chat with Keith Todd, John Bird, Brian Purcell, Roy Evans, Ivor Allchurch and Alan Jones.

113. It's October 1960 and Hibernian play in front of a packed Vetch crowd to celebrate the arrival of floodlighting.

114. End of an era. Ivor Allchurch walks off the Vetch Field pitch for the last time surrounded by hundreds of admiring schoolboys after his testimonial in May 1968.

115. Farewell, too, for Joe Sykes and the turn-out for this benefit game in 1968 shows what the top players thought of the club's father figure. The star studded line-up is *standing, from left to right:* Ivor Allchurch, Bryn Jones, Terry Medwin, Ken Evans, Ray Daniel, Roy Paul, Dai James, John Charles, Jack Parry, Reg Davies, Mel Nurse, Norman Lawson, Ivor Powell, Billy Lucas, Trevor Ford. *front:* Roy Saunders, Harry Griffiths, Peter Davies, Cliff Jones, Mel Charles, Tom Kiley, Vic Gomersall.

116. Tea break and Dolly Phillips dishes it out to Jimmy McLaughlin, Vic Gomersall, John Roberts, Brian Purcell and apprentice Billy Beer.

117. Ball control, demonstrated basketball fashion by Brian Hughes, Peter Davies, Brayley Reynolds, Reg Davies, Harry Griffiths and Roy Saunders.

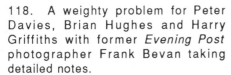

118. A weighty problem for Peter Davies, Brian Hughes and Harry Griffiths with former *Evening Post* photographer Frank Bevan taking detailed notes.

119. Team talk conducted by manager Trevor Morris with one or two players clearly seeing the funny side of the camera's presence.

120. Looking more like the beach Harry Griffiths gets a helping hand over the unfamiliar terrain from Johnny King while Alan Sanders jogs alongside.

121. Munich air crash survivor Ken Morgans is welcomed to the Vetch by Barrie Jones, Roy Saunders, Len Allchurch, Harry Griffiths, Mel Nurse and manager Trevor Morris after his transfer from Manchester United in 1960.

122. Another triumph, this time in the Welsh Cup, and Peter Davies, Mel Nurse, Herbie Williams, Harry Griffiths, Barrie Jones and Peter Donnelly join in the celebrations.

123. Dixie Hale, three goals in 34 League games 1959-61.

124. David Dodson, 12 goals in 31 League games 1959-62.

125. Derek Draper, 10 goals in 62 League games 1962-66.

126. Joe Davis signs for the Swans, March 1967, watched by new manager Billy Lucas.

127. Left-back Dai Ward made 46 League appearances 1960-66.

128. Full-back David Lawrence, following in the footsteps of father Syd who captained the club in the thirties.

129. History makers ... Swansea win the Welsh Cup in 1960 and earn the right to become the first Welsh club to play in Europe. Mel Nurse holds the trophy watched by among others Barrie Jones, Graham Williams, Brayleu Reynolds, Peter Davies, Roy Saunders , Reg Davies, Harry Griffiths and manager Trevor Morris.

Back from the Brink

Swansea was still very much a depressed soccer area when the new board took over. Despite early success under new manager Roy Bentley, the pre Toshack era was punctuated regularly with gloom, despondency and great controversy.

Not least among the major issues of the day was the decision midway through the 1974-75 season to sell the ground, the club's one main asset, to the local authority.

Swansea had an overdraft of £150,000, bank charges had risen to £14,000 and efforts to find a solution to the worsening financial crisis by developing the North Bank site and linking it in with the city's Quadrant scheme received a firm thumbs down.

With land prices rising, the Vetch Field was estimated to be worth around £1 million - but only to developers and not to the city council while they continued to allow Swansea to play League football.

Having been refused permission to develop part of the ground, the board felt it had no alternative other than to sell it to the council who paid £200,000, which included a highly controversial grant of £150,000 that had to be used solely to discharge the bank overdraft.

A further clause in the agreement meant that if Swansea went out of the League, the club had to surrender the lease. The city fathers must have had clairvoyant powers. At the end of the season, Swansea sank to the lowest point in its history when the club was forced to re-apply for re-election.

Prior to the League's annual meeting, chairman Malcolm Struel and Harry Griffiths, by now manager after several months as caretaker since the resignation of Harry Gregg, compiled a letter which was sent to the other 91 League clubs. The plea from the heart, coupled with a good deal of canvassing by manager and chairman, did the trick. Swansea achieved the largest number of votes among the four clubs seeking to stay in the League.

No-one could have predicted quite such a dramatic slide after the early success under Bentley who steered Swansea out of the Fourth Division in 1969-70 - his first season.

The return of Len Allchurch and the arrival of Welsh international goalkeeper Tony Millington from Peterborough proved significant captures. Allchurch and Brian Evans carved out the openings, and David Gwyther with 22 goals and Herbie Williams (17) missed few scoring opportunities. Add the commanding presence of Nurse in the heart of the defence and the brilliance of Millington, and it was little wonder that Swansea never felt in awe when they met mighty Leeds in the FA Cup at Elland Road. Swansea led through Gwyther until the second half when the tie swung dramatically after Nurse was sent off.

By the end of the promotion season, Swansea had blooded Dai Davies but his stay in the first team was brief. Everton spotted his potential so Swansea, with Millington an able deputy, sold their young goalkeeper for £20,000. Swansea had added the experience of Barrie Hole, £20,000 from Aston Villa, and Len Hill, £5,000 from Newport, to stiffen their Third Division challenge. Hole's arrival maintained a strong family link. He was the third of Billy Hole's sons to play for the club. Despite his stylish presence, Swansea struggled until they put together a 19-match unbeaten League run, equalling a club record, to haul themselves up to 11th place with the help of 27-goal Gwyther. The double retirement of Nurse and Len Allchurch weakened Swansea hopes of building on that run. Bentley rigorously pursued his policy of giving youngsters a chance but the most significant capture came in July 1972 when Alan Curtis, a nephew of Roy Paul, became an apprentice.

Swansea had by then added Welsh international winger Ronnie Rees to the side, but the record £26,000 signing failed to make the impact expected. Hole's retirement left a big gap as well after a season when Swansea lost £25,000. Within a few months of the start of the 1972-73 season, Bentley resigned after Malcolm Struel had taken over as chairman from David Goldstone.

For a new manager Swansea turned to former Northern Ireland goalkeeper Harry Gregg, a survivor of the Munich air disaster, but it proved a disastrous appointment.

During Gregg's reign the club had the worst disciplinary record in its history, its lowest gate (1,301 against Northampton) and the poorest record since the thirties. Within five months of his arrival Swansea were back in the Fourth Division.

Swansea, £100,000 in debt, sold Brian Evans to Hereford for £7,000 and David Gwyther to Halifax for £12,000, reinvesting the money by recruiting Danny Bartley and Dave Bruton in a £10,000 deal with Bristol City and paying £8,000 to York for Pat Lally.

The changes failed to produce a significant improvement in fortunes and the only bright spot on the horizon was the emergence of Robbie James and Curtis and the brilliance of Jimmy Rimmer, on loan from Gregg's old club, Manchester United.

Just prior to Gregg's inevitable departure Herbie Williams left to take up a player-coach appointment in Australia after playing more than 500 League games and scoring over 100 goals in a career which stretched from 1958 to 1975.

Perhaps the final indictment on Gregg's reign was that a defender, Wyndham Evans, finished top scorer with nine goals, a situation which changed dramatically after Griffiths had assumed control.

Griffiths, also charged with improving the club's appalling disciplinary record, achieved both tasks with the help of Geoff Bray, a striker signed from Oxford, former Brighton winger Micky Conway, whose career was cut short by a car accident, and, probably the most significant signing, experienced midfielder George Smith from Cardiff. With two other important recruits, Eddie May and Les Chappell, adding experience in defence and midfield, Griffiths had assembled a side capable of matching the best in the Fourth Division.

The innovative manager made other changes, converting Bartley from a winger to a full back; midfielder Geoff Thomas into a sweeper; and pushing Curtis forward from midfield.

Griffiths also benefitted from the emergence of the latest member of the Charles clan, Mel's 16 year old son Jeremy, at a time when his uncle John Charles resigned as youth team manager.

Charles junior scored two goals on a dream debut against Newport in the League Cup and finished the season with 26 in all competitions as Swansea rattled in a club record 92 League goals, just missing out on promotion despite winning the last game of the season at Cambridge.

Sadly, when Swansea finally made it, Griffiths, having laid such solid foundations, would not be around to savour the moment.

130. Herbie Williams scores his 100th goal for the club.

131. Back in the Third Division: the team which clinched promotion in 1970. *back row, from left to right:* Carl Slee, Alan Williams, Herbie Williams, Tony Millington, David Gwyther, Geoff Thomas, Vic Gomersall. *seated:* Len Allchurch, David Lawrence, Mel Nurse, Brian Evans, Billy Screen.

132. Herbie Williams scores his 100th goal for the club and the *Evening Post* marks the occasion when Sports Editor Bill Paton hands over a framed reminder of the goal captured by photographer Len Pitson. Looking on in the Vetch Field treatment room are physiotherapist Bernard Cherrington (*centre*) and manager Roy Bentley.

133. Geoff Thomas outjumps the Liverpool defence but Swansea lost this 1970-71 FA Cup tie.

1. Len Allchurch who joined the club straight from school and had two spells with Swansea.

II. Ready for action at the start of the 1975-76 season. *standing:* Roy Saunders (coach), Nigel Stevenson, Jeremy Charles, Gary Moore, Eddie May, Steve Potter, Keith Barber, Dave Bruton, Neil Davids, Robbie James, Jeff Griffiths, Stephen Morris, Harry Griffiths (manager). *in front:* Micky Conway, Les Chappell, Pat Lally, Alan Curtis, George Smith (captain), Wyndham Evans, Danny Bartley, Nigel Dalling, Kevin Moore.

NORTH ENDER

THE OFFICIAL PROGRAMME OF PRESTON NORTH END FOOTBALL CLUB SEASON 1980/81

FOOTBALL LEAGUE DIVISION TWO
PRESTON NORTH END
v
SWANSEA CITY

Saturday, 2nd May, 1981   Kick-off 3-00 p.m.

Match Sponsor: GARRATT SON & FLOWERDEW LTD

BE PROUD TO

SWANSEA CITY F.C.

BE A SWAN

the Swan

EUROPEAN CUP WINNERS CUP
FIRST ROUND/FIRST LEG

FC Lokomotiv Leipzig

WEDNESDAY, 16th SEPTEMBER, 1981
Kick-Off 7.30 p.m.

35p

TOSH ★ ABOUT THE OPPOSITION ★ PRESS BOX
CHAIRMAN'S MESSAGE ★ DAVID FARMER
WALES IN EUROPE ★ NEWS DESK
FLASHBACK ★ LEIGHTON JAMES

VI. Striker Alan Curtis weaves his way through the Ipswich defence during the 1981-82 meeting at Vetch Field.

VII. In possession ... Ray Kennedy with Manchester City's Asa Hartford waiting to pounce.

VIII. The determination shows as Swansea's Gary Stanley and Manchester City's Peter Barnes contest the loose ball.

IX. Yugoslav Dzemal Hadziabdic dwarfed by a section of the East Stand.

X. On his own ... Alan Curtis.

XI. Chris Marustik slips the ball under a sliding challenge from Asa Hartford.

XII. Yugoslav Dzemal Hadziabdic is stopped in his tracks.

XIII. First Division Swansea City pose with the Welsh Cup.

XIV. Start of another season and bronzed John Toshack poses with the silver Welsh Cup.

XV. Colin Irwin, signed for a club record of £350,000, had his playing career cut short by an horrific injury in a game at Aston Villa.

the Swan

BE PROUD TO

SWANSEA CITY F.C.

BE A SWAN

35p

WELSH CUP FINAL · SECOND LEG
CARDIFF CITY
WEDNESDAY, 19th MAY, 1982

EDITORIAL ★ TOSH ★ PHOTOS ★ PRO-FILE ★ FLASHBACK
OUR VISITORS ★ DAVID FARMER ★ PRESS BOX
STATISTICS ★ TONY PULLEIN ★ GEOFF FORD
TONY HOWARD ★ LES CHAPPELL

XVII. Perfectly poised ... Swansea winger Leighton James.

XVIII. Racing clear ... Robbie James supported by Ray
Kennedy.

The Swan

BE PROUD TO

SWANSEA CITY F.C.

BE A SWAN

EUROPEAN CUP WINNERS CUP - Preliminary Round

SPORTING BRAGA

TUESDAY. 17th AUGUST. 1982
Kick-off 7.30 pm

35p

With the Compliments of
LEWBRAID
Aluminium Windows Limited
and
LEWBRAID
Aluminium Seamless Gutters Limited

Swansea City FC Fixture List 1982/83

**LAST SEASON'S MOST CONSISTENT
FIRST DIVISION TEAM**

XXII. Back in the Second Division but everyone looks cheerful at the start of the 1983-84 season.

Swansea City FC Financial Appeal Game

SWANSEA CITY
v
MANCHESTER UTD.

MONDAY, 13th JANUARY, 1986   Kick-Off 7.30 pm

SOUVENIR PROGRAMME £1

Welcome to the Vetch

BARCLAYS LEAGUE DIVISION 4

The SWAN

PLAY OFFS - FINAL FIRST LEG

TORQUAY

WEDNESDAY, 25th MAY, 1988
Kick Off 7.30 p.m.

SPONSORED BY DIVERSIFIED PRODUCTS

Fit for Life   50p

OFFICIAL PROGRAMME

XXV. The long serving Wyndham Evans, released, recalled, and released again. Wyndham played more than 350 League games for the Swans.

134. Manager Harry Griffiths welcomes new signing George Smith while the rest of the flared set look on.

135. Tony Millington, 178 League games.

136. Cap that ... from the youth team right through to the senior Wales team, Robbie James, Jeremy Charles, Alan Curtis, Nigel Stevenson.

137. Dream debut. Jeremy Charles scores his second goal against Newport in August 1976.

138. Glen Davies, 152 League games 1970-76.

139. Centre half Eddie May, 90 League games 1976-78.

140. No stopping David Gwyther as he scores against Rhyl in the Welsh Cup.

141. Pat Lally, 160 League games 1973-79.

142. Defender Dave Bruton, 193 League games 1973-79.

143-145. *left:* Striker Andy Leitch came back to the Vetch to knock his old club out of the FA Cup as a Minehead player. *centre:* Danny Bartley, 199 League appearances 1973-80. *right:* Striker Gary Moore, eight goals in 34 League games 1976-78.

The Golden Years

Triumph and Tragedy

By the early weeks of 1978 Swansea were relentlessly pursuing a new manager to tackle the rebuilding process, begun by the popular Harry Griffiths, a stage further.

Griffiths was still in charge, but the pressures of the job coupled with his own misgivings over how much further he could take Swansea led to the growing belief that a younger man was needed.

Swansea had already been turned down by Colin Addison, Bill McGarry and Eddie McCreadie and seemed no nearer ending their quest when they were given a helping hand from the unlikeliest of us. Cardiff were struggling near the bottom of the Second Division and John Toshack's career at Liverpool was over. A marriage between the capital city and its favourite son seemed inevitable.

Instead, Toshack left Ninian Park shaking his head in disbelief at the lack of ambition shown by his old club, and made his way to Swansea where he spent the rest of the day working for a London-based firm at a sports exhibition.

Managing Fourth Division Swansea could not have been further from his thoughts as he chatted to Barry John about his future. Before the day was out Viv Jenkins, a business associate of the Welsh rugby international, had set up a meeting with Swansea chairman Malcolm Struel and the seeds of a partnership which were to carry Swansea to the top of the First Division were sown.

Swansea had already underlined the ambitions which appealed to Toshack by turning down a £165,000 bid from Sunderland for Alan Curtis. Sunderland manager, Jimmy Adamson would land his man later when he moved to Leeds but in the meantime there was a job to finish at Swansea. Appropriately Toshack started work on St David's Day and promotion was on the cards provided he could motivate the players. With 16 games left, Swansea could afford few mistakes, but Toshack decided to pin everything on the combined attacking talents of Curtis, Robbie James, Jeremy Charles and himself. It worked like a dream from the moment Toshack made his debut against Watford in front of more than 16,000 - treble the average gate.

Toshack's arrival from Liverpool's medal winning team generated so much interest that the figure never fell below 7,000 for the rest of the season. The results from Swansea's entertaining style of play had a lot to do with that as well. Hartlepool discovered that. They were on the wrong end of an 8-0 scoreline, Swansea's biggest League triumph, which produced hat-tricks for top marksmen Curtis and James.

With five matches left Swansea were lying fourth, but even after losing at Grimsby and

Northampton they still had a three-point cushion. Two home wins over Scunthorpe and Halifax, with Toshack scoring in both games, finally clinched promotion in front of another 16,000 crowd.

But the celebrations were soured by the tragic death of Harry Griffiths on the morning of the Scunthorpe match. More than anyone he had helped to reshape Swansea after re-election and made everyone sit up and take notice of the Swansea side which topped the League goal charts two seasons running. The show, of course, still went on but there was no doubt who the players were performing for on that emotional Vetch Field night.

Sadly, on the day when the cheering never stopped, the man who wanted to be there joining in was missing, but the Harry Griffiths room, decorated with *Evening Post* photographs is a permanent reminder of his long and distinguished service to the club.

The Liverpool Connection

Every manager will tell you that the close season can make or break a team and, judging by Toshack's first summer in management, he had evidently learned a lot from his Anfield mentor Bill Shankly.

After the inevitable "will he, won't he" saga surrounding the club's hottest property, Alan Curtis signed a new one-year contract while Toshack put the £50,000 he had to spend on new players to good use.

First he paid Leicester £20,000 for his old Anfield understudy Alan Waddle, which reunited two of the tallest strikers in British football, and then splashed out £25,000 for Crewe goalkeeper Geoff Crudgington.

Both players were to have a significant impact on that new Third Division season, but it was the arrival of Tommy Smith and Ian Callaghan which set the tongues wagging and installed Swansea up among the championship favourites.

Smith had been playing for Los Angeles Aztecs and Callaghan for Fort Lauderdale Strikers. The double swoop provided the kind of experience money could not buy and cemented the Liverpool link which would get stronger over the coming seasons.

Toshack, a professional down to his bootlaces, was determined to get the backroom structure right as well and he brought in Terry Medwin, an old Vetch Field favourite, as his assistant. Professionalism was the name of the game and with Smith carrying the added responsibility of captaincy, Swansea thrived on the Third Division challenge.

Just how good this emerging Swansea team was, Tottenham discovered in a Football League Cup tie at Vetch Field, hyped up by the first appearance in Wales of Argentina's World Cup heroes Osvaldo

Ardiles and Ricardo Villa. More than 24,000 watched the tie which will be remembered just as much for Smith's first minute tackle on the gifted Ardiles as the entertaining football which produced a 2-2 draw. The Smith-Ardiles confrontation almost became an international incident and no-one really gave Swansea much chance in the replay at White Hart Lane. On the night everything went right. Toshack, playing as a sweeper, out-manoeuvred Spurs manager Keith Burkinshaw and Swansea romped home 3-1.

The growing Anfield influence was further strengthened by the arrival of Phil Boersma for a record £30,000 fee from Luton. The transfer record was broken again before Christmas when Toshack paid Aston Villa £70,000 for Welsh international defender Leighton Phillips. It all helped to strengthen the growing belief that a return to the Second Division was possible, but again it was to be achieved at a price.

With seven matches left, Boersma suffered a compound fracture of his right ankle at Swindon, an injury which effectively finished his career. It was a tragic blow to club and player, but again Swansea had to apply themselves to the job in hand and no-one could have scripted things better as Swansea went into the last match of the season against Chesterfield needing a win to end 14 years exile from the Second Division. Needless to say it was an emotional night but the highly charged atmosphere was almost dampened when Chesterfield snatched the lead from a corner.

Even though Alan Waddle equalised Swansea struggled to break through again until Toshack left the substitute's bench to score the goal that clinched promotion. He laid the credit for it at the feet of John Charles from whom he had learned so much when he was a Cardiff apprentice, and that generous tribute endeared him even more to the Swansea public.

The History Makers

The celebrations were still going on when Toshack faced up to the first of many close season headaches - the future of Alan Curtis.

Swansea had held the big clubs at bay during two promotion seasons, but could not refuse a deal which would net the club £350,000. Swansea had tried desperately to persuade their highly rated striker to stay but within days of arriving in the Second Division Curtis was on his way to Leeds, at the time the most expensive British player outside the First Division. While Toshack was clearly disappointed by the loss of such a valued player the cash from the departure of Curtis provided the funds to strengthen his squad for the Second Division challenge. Tommy Craig (£150,000 from Aston Villa), John Mahoney (£100,000 from Middlesbrough) and Dave Rushbury (£60,000 from Sheffield Wednesday) provided additional experience during what was very much a transitional season.

Despite that settling in period attendances never dropped below 10,000 but Toshack probably knew early in the season that it would need a winter for the team and himself to readjust after two heady promotion campaigns. The rebuilding never stopped, but for the first time Toshack was finding it increasingly difficult combining the dual role of player and manager. He was playing less and less, but still kept busy in the transfer market trying to find the right balance and blend for his Second Division team. Neil Robinson (£70,000) arrived from Everton and David Giles, for a similar fee, was bought from Wrexham. But the biggest headache was finding a goalkeeper. After successive defeats Swansea axed Crudgington and paid Chesterfield £50,000 for Glan Letheren who was not the success Toshack had hoped. After selling Crudgington to Plymouth, Dave Stewart arrived from West Bromwich Albion and kept his place in the side until Swansea climbed into the First Division 15 months later.

Perhaps the most significant capture came three days before the end of the season when Swansea paid Burnley £120,000 for Leighton James who repaid the first instalment in the last match of the season at Charlton, scoring one goal and making the other in a winning debut as a second half substitute.

Swansea had already unveiled ambitious plans to give the Vetch Field a facelift, but Toshack continued to concentrate his efforts on building a team to challenge for a place in the First Division. Signing the brilliant Welsh international winger was a significant step along that road. Another came in August when the club made its boldest capture - Dzemal Hadziabdic, signed for £160,000 after an emotional debut in a friendly fixture against Tottenham

The match attracted nearly 12,000 and for an hour the Yugoslav full back treated the public to a glimpse of the attacking flair which was to prove so influential during the next nine months.

That historic 1980-81 season started slowly and Toshack was to regret not selling David Giles to Crystal Palace for £400,000 when he had the opportunity at the end of the previous season. Giles had been an outstanding success in his short stay at the club, but was never able to maintain that early consistency. Eventually he did move to Selhurst Park in a part exchange deal which brought Ian Walsh to Swansea.

Despite that sluggish start Swansea quickly put together several unbeaten runs which suggested to that wise old sage Bill Shankly that his young protege had what he described as the recipe.

By mid December Swansea were lying fourth, but the return of Alan Curtis following a miserable 18 months at Elland Road was to prove one of the turning points of the season.

Even Toshack, however, had doubts about the side's ability to stay in the promotion race, so in January he took the players off to Spain for a mid winter break. It should have been just the tonic, but on their return the club promptly lost the next four League games. So much for Mediterranean sun.

Shortly afterwards, Swansea enlisted another Yugoslav, Ante Rajkovic, but the true value of the

£100,000 invested would not be seen until the following season.

Much more pressing was a problem concerning Leighton Phillips, who was so upset at being left out of the side for the friendly against Red Star Belgrade that he asked for a transfer. Although manager and player patched things up it was clear that Swansea had a problem in the heart of the defence where the accomplished Phillips had been operating as a sweeper. After much soul searching Toshack entrusted the job to Dudley Lewis, the youth team captain. It proved an inspired choice, another part of the Toshack legend which reached a heady climax at Preston on 2 May 1981 when the club reached the First Division.

Swansea, lying seventh with nine matches left, hauled themselves back into the hunt with an unbeaten run but had a let-off in the final home match against Luton who came close to spoiling the celebrations. Ten thousand fans turned Deepdale into a home match and Swansea, with goals from Leighton James, Tommy Craig and Jeremy Charles, were carried to victory on a sea of black and white scarves. Lewis was still there on that unforgettable day. He was the first player Toshack congratulated after the club had completed the journey from the Fourth Division in a record four seasons. He was still in school when it started, but there were four playing members who had been in the side from the start, Wyndham Evans, Robbie James, Alan Curtis and Jeremy Charles, and perhaps it was fitting that three of them, James, Curtis and Charles, were involved in the last goal at Preston.

To complete a memorable season Swansea lifted the Welsh Cup as well for the first time since 1966, a feat which was to be repeated three years running. With that success came a passage into Europe but the attraction of playing in the Cup-Winners' Cup proved a big let down. Only once did Swansea reach the second round and then it was after beating mediocre opposition.

Still, Swansea were in the First Division for the first time in their history. That really was the prize after four remarkable seasons and to think that none of it would have been possible if Cardiff had shown the foresight to snap up their favourite son when they had the chance.

146. Tension mounts on the faces of John Toshack and Phil Boersma in the Deepdale dug-out on that May day in 1981 when Swansea climbed into the First Division.

147-149. Thousands line the streets of Swansea to salute the First Division's newest arrivals.

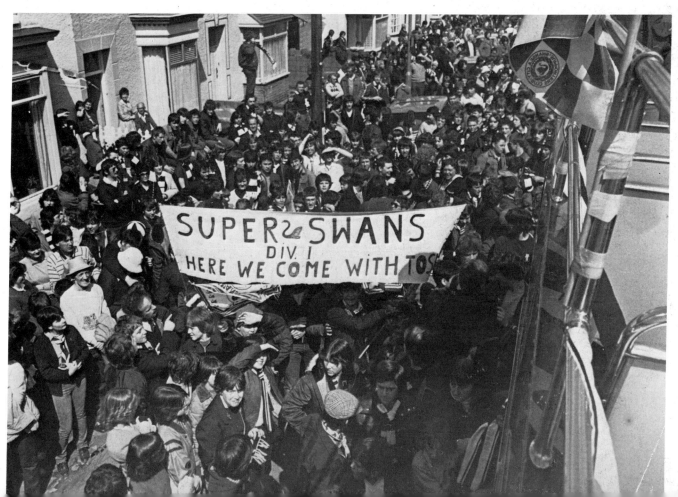

150. At the Vetch the players thank the fans for their support.

151. No lap of honour for Nigel Stevenson. He played on at Preston despite damaging an ankle which had to be put in plaster after the match. Tommy Craig, Wyndham Evans, Robbie James, Dzemal Hadziabdic, Neil Robinson and Leighton James examine the extent of the injury.

152. Double celebrations ... Swansea follow promotion to the First Division by lifting the Welsh Cup.

South Wales Evening Post

LATE SPORTS FINAL

No. 33,567   SATURDAY, MAY 2, 1981   10p

Preston 1 . . . Swansea City 3

FIRST DIVISION

By John Burgum

SWANSEA CITY will be playing First Division football next season for the first time since they joined the Football League 60 years ago.

John Toshack's team clinched promotion in dramatic fashion at Preston this afternoon, the last Saturday of the season, and at the same time carved a place in British soccer's hall of fame.

No club in the history of the game has swept from the Fourth Division to the First with such speed and style.

It's taken Swansea just three years to complete the climb, after surviving a re-election application in 1975 and being forced to rebuild virtually from scratch.

Three survivors from that low point in the club's history, Wyndham Evans, Alan Curtis and Robbie James, were still around today for the climax of a remarkable rags to riches transformation.

The reshaping though has been in no small measure due to boardroom ambition and the arrival three years ago of Toshack.

Persuading Toshack to leave his beloved Liverpool to enter League management has turned into a master stroke.

Two successive promotion seasons, a return to Europe after an absence of 15 years and now the First Division.

The scope seems endless for a manager who at 32 has become one of the most respected in his profession.

Toshack's contribution has been considerable but right at the heart of the success story has been a spirited team effort involving all sections of a thriving club.

Directors, players, management backroom staff . . . everyone can take pride in Swansea's finest achievement.

Swansea have come a long way since they were admitted as founder members of the Third Division in 1920.

Next season they can look forward to having such great club sides as Liverpool, Ipswich, Manchester United and Arsenal on their fixture list.

The First Division has arrived — and now everyone can start that champagne celebration.

● Preston v. Swansea match report — see Page 3.

CLIMBING TO THE HEIGHTS . . . Swansea goalkeeper Dave Stewart cuts out a cross at Deepdale today as Nigel Stevenson watches anxiously.

154. Ian Callaghan, such a major influence during the Third Division promotion campaign.

155. Yugoslav Dzemal Hadziabdic, the first continental player to be imported by a Welsh club. Everyone called the popular full back Jimmy. His vocabulary was limited but he was far more expressive on the field.

156. John Toshack scores with a spectacular flying header against Hull.

157. Familiar sight, Toshack scoring in the 4-2 win over Sheffield Wednesday.

158A-C. *left:* Ray Kennedy, a major disappointment after a distinguished career with Arsenal and Liverpool. *centre:* Yugoslav defender Ante Rajkovic was a tower of strength when Swansea arrived in the First Division. *right:* First Division goalkeeper Dai Davies, back where he started his career.

First Division - Too Much Too Soon

Somehow the euphoria never stopped during that heady summer of 1981 as Swansea prepared to meet the new competitive demands of the First Division. No matter where you turned or what newspaper you read, Swansea always seemed to creep into the conversation and the headlines.

Capacity gates were predicted and money seemed no object at a club which was determined to compete with the best in the land. The reality of the situation was very different and that high cost was to prove Swansea's downfall. No one knew it then, of course, as Toshack embarked on a necessary spending spree to strengthen his relatively inexperienced squad.

For many of the players under Toshack's wing the First Division was unchartered territory. Fortunately the manager had spent the best part of his career there and with £500,000 available for new players, he knew the importance of signing performers of proven ability.

With a goalkeeper, defender and a striker on his shopping list, he toyed with the idea of putting in a bid for his former Liverpool team mate Ray Clemence. When the budget would not stretch to meet the £300,000 needed to recruit the England goalkeeper, Swansea signed Wales choice Dai Davies. Despite some criticism of his early performances after joining the Vetch Field staff at £45,000, Davies proved a bargain buy.

The same is true for Bob Latchford. The former England striker cost £125,000 but was one of Swansea's most consistent players during what was to prove an all too brief encounter with the First Division.

For the defender he needed, Toshack went back to Anfield to recruit Colin Irwin for a club record £350,000, an inflated price for a player of promise with limited first team experience. Irwin was handed the captaincy, in the same way as another Anfield player, Tommy Smith, had a few seasons earlier. He hardly missed a game during that memorable first season when visits to Old Trafford, Highbury, White Hart Lane and Anfield replaced those seemingly monotonous trips to Halifax, Crewe, Stockport and Rochdale where Toshack had watched his first Swansea match.

However, even with three new players, few could have predicted the outcome as Swansea's million pound team lined up against Leeds United on that historic August day when the club made its First Division debut. Even now the scoreline takes some believing - Swansea 5 Leeds 1 - a match watched by almost 24,000 which set the tone for a season which saw Swansea top the First Division on three separate occasions.

More significantly, perhaps, the Championship was a possibility following a superb nine-match unbeaten run in the New Year, but Swansea lost two crucial home matches against Ipswich and West Ham and had to settle for sixth spot after tailing off badly, losing five of their last six League matches.

Still, no one was complaining on that first day against Leeds when Latchford scored a hat-trick in nine minutes thirteen seconds, one of the quickest on record and the fastest by a Swansea player.

On top of that Jeremy Charles, second generation member of the famous Swansea footballing family, scored the club's first goal in the First Division but the best on that historic day came from Alan Curtis who could not contain his delight at scoring against his old club.

By the time Swansea's brief flirtation with European football was coming to a swift conclusion against the disciplined East Germans from Lokomotiv Leipzig, Toshack had added two more players to his ambitious First Division squad: Gary Stanley, signed from Everton for £150,000; and Max Thompson, a £20,000 buy from Blackpool.

That trip behind the Iron Curtain, however, was marred by the death of Bill Shankly, from whom Toshack had learned so much, first as a player, then a manager. Ironically the next match was at Anfield where both had built their reputation. Toshack underlined just how much he owed to Shankly and the respect he had for him by wearing a Liverpool No 10 jersey during the minute silence before the game and then going over to the Kop end of the ground after Swansea had been forced to settle for a 2-2 draw after leading 2-0. That did not go down too well with the Swansea public but Toshack shrewdly redressed the balance in the next home match by revealing a Swansea No 10 jersey before the game.

A few weeks later Swansea were sitting proudly on top of the First Division for the first time, having won at Stoke after announcing a loss of £270,000. It was the tip of a large and very threatening financial iceberg.

Swansea had been dumped out of the League Cup by Barnsley when they went to Ipswich to produce what many still regard as one of their finest First Division performances, winning a memorable game 3-2 in front of England manager Ron Greenwood.

Having dropped to third place, Swansea were back on top again at Christmas, beating Jimmy Rimmer's League Champions Aston Villa 2-1 at Vetch Field with two goals from Robbie James.

Kevin Keegan spoiled any prospect of lengthy celebrations by destroying Swansea almost single-handed at Southampton before Liverpool handed out a further lesson in the FA Cup at Vetch Field. Swansea had lost their way and Toshack responded by going back to his old club Liverpool to sign Ray Kennedy for £160,000 amid one report suggesting he was going to sign for Sunderland for half that fee. At the time it seemed just the lift the side needed, but it proved a disastrous signing. Kennedy never settled and after problems on and off the field, he eventually had his contract cancelled by mutual consent. His stay cost the club more than £3,000 per appearance.

Despite one or two New Year hiccups - among them a second knee operation for Charles - Swansea quickly avenged their Cup defeat by beating Liverpool 2-0 at Vetch Field with late goals from Leighton James and Alan Curtis to stay in the top six.

Ian Walsh arrived from Crystal Palace with David Giles going the other way without any money changing hands. Kennedy scored on a winning return to Highbury and, on 20 March, Swansea were back on top of the table again after Walsh had scored the winner at Wolves.

March was significant for another reason as well. During the space of four days Swansea had 13 players on international duty at various levels, six of them in Spain with the senior squad where Chris Marustik made his debut.

Back home Dave Stewart was offered a free transfer but as Swansea kept up the Championship chase the pressure started to show. Wins over West Brom, Southampton and Manchester City kept the club in touch, but five defeats in the last six matches killed off any prospect of a dream finish to the club's top flight debut.

Five teenagers - Dudley Lewis, Jimmy Loveridge, Chris Sander, Gary Richards and Darren Gale - made their First Division bow in the last match at Villa Park but already some shrewd observers were suggesting that Swansea were in for an uncomfortable ride next time around. How right they were as the 1982-83 season set Swansea on a rather different journey and almost out of existence as a League club.

It started promisingly enough. Success in Europe was followed by wins over Norwich and Coventry before the cracks appeared with four successive defeats.

By September it became clear why Swansea had not strengthened the side. The Football League had banned them from buying new players because they had fallen behind in their payments for the £150,000 it had cost them to sign Gary Stanley from Everton and the club still owed Liverpool money for Kennedy and Irwin. With gates dropping well below the 18,000 first season average trouble was just around the corner.

Swansea's problems were not helped by an injury Irwin suffered at Aston Villa which effectively finished his career. Swansea's record signing snapped the patela tendon in his right knee but even though he played in the club's final match in the First

159. Setting off in the First Division. *back row, left to right:* David Giles, Dave Rushbury, Dudley Lewis, Dave Stewart, Dai Davies, Ante Rajkovic, Leighton James. *middle:* Phil Boersma, assistant manager, John Mahoney, Brian Attley, Neil Robinson, Chris Marustik, Dzemal Hadziabdic, Tommy Craig, Doug Livermore, coach. *seated:* Jeremy Charles, Nigel Stevenson, Alan Curtis, John Toshack, manager, Wyndham Evans, Robbie James, Bob Latchford.

Division his promising career was over.

By November Swansea were out of the Cup-Winners' Cup, beaten by Paris St Germain, and then suffered the humiliation of going out of the Milk Cup to Third Division Brentford before the full cost of the club's success was revealed in accounts which showed Swansea almost £2 million in debt.

Now Swansea were making headlines of a very different kind. Kennedy was relieved of the captaincy and suspended from the club for two weeks while Leighton James, such an influence during Swansea's climb out of the Second Division, went on a free transfer to Sunderland.

On top of that Toshack was banned from the touchline for four months after being found guilty of bringing the game into disrepute, and as the pressure mounted it became increasingly evident that Swansea were putting their faith in younger players.

Swansea offered Stanley for sale at £30,000 - evidence of how the bottom had fallen out of the transfer market; Latchford turned down a move to Chelsea; injuries robbed the side of Hadziabdic and Mahoney; Kennedy was put on the transfer list; Dai Davies was told his contract would not be renewed and Swansea persevered with youngsters who simply did not have either the knowledge or experience to keep Swansea in the First Division.

Swansea's flickering hopes were finally extinguished by Bryan Robson at Old Trafford and the club were back in the Second Division after just two seasons.

Twelve months later they were in the Third Division but by then Robbie James, player of the year in that first season in the top flight, had gone to Stoke and his departure meant that the transfer embargo was lifted long enough to sign Jimmy Rimmer from Aston Villa.

By the end of September 1983 Swansea were bottom of the Second Division without a win in five League games; former England captain Emlyn Hughes signed a three month contract; Mahoney was forced to retire because of injury; Latchford and Marustik wanted to leave and Charles was put up for sale before the growing unrest within the boardroom ended with the resignation of chairman Malcolm Struel and vice chairman Tom Phillips.

Doug Sharpe took over as chairman as the financial crisis deepened and top earners like Kennedy, Latchford, Walsh, Curtis, Stanley and Robinson were all made available.

With Swansea needing to find £400,000 immediately to satisfy creditors the future looked bleak. Kennedy was paid off and then Toshack resigned as manager of the club he had carried to the top of the First Division. It was the end of an era but not Toshack's association with the club. Fifty-three days later he was invited back to take charge

160. The camera captures a piece of history, Swansea's first goal in Division One scored by Jeremy Charles who finds the target, watches the goalkeeper dive in vain and then turns to a cheering crowd.

after his successor Doug Livermore had quit and Colin Appleton, to whom approaches had been made, had decided to remain with Hull. By then, however, Swansea had raised around £170,000 by selling Charles and Curtis and within days of Toshack's return, Swansea had given free transfers to Latchford, Stanley and newcomer Gary Chivers.

So in the space of a year Swansea parted company with Leighton James, Robbie James, Dai Davies, Yugoslavs Ante Rajkovic and Dzemal Hadziabdic, Alan Curtis, Jeremy Charles, Max Thompson, Ray Kennedy and, albeit briefly, Wyndham Evans - the player Toshack summoned back from Welsh League football as his player-coach when he returned for a second stint as manager.

Survival was uppermost in Toshack's thoughts and the sentiments in the boardroom were much the same. Even though Swansea had slashed their wage bill by 50 per cent they promised to cut it again and promptly put Rimmer up for sale.

Owing the Inland Revenue more than £100,000 Swansea offered to pay by instalments to head off a High Court hearing, but another row was brewing when Doug Sharpe fired Toshack in March after he had refused to resign following a string of poor results. It prompted a torrid public debate between Messrs Struel and Sharpe - the first in a long series of such outbursts between various factions over the next two years which took the emphasis away from

what was happening on the field and helped to bring the club to its knees.

Amid this backdrop of constant bickering the aimiable Les Chappell took over as caretaker manager with ambitions to make the job permanent. The players liked his compassionate approach but the board, ignoring a petition from the players, had other ideas.

Swansea, already doomed to a second successive relegation season, announced a £600,000 loss in April 1984 and the balance sheet for the second season in the First Division revealed that the club was £2 million in the red. The decline was almost as dramatic as the club's remarkable rise to prominence. Success had come too quickly and Swansea were paying a heavy price for too much too soon.

Where Did It All Go Wrong?

There was no single reason, but several, linked to the collapse. The club, anticipating capacity gates when they arrived in the First Division, went on a spending spree which helped to sow the seeds of its own destruction.

As part of a £2 million investment programme they signed big name players at inflated prices, gave them huge wages and clearly hoped to recoup the outlay through the turnstiles and a thriving

161. Bob Latchford scores the first goal in a nine-minute hat-trick against Leeds.

commercial department.

Swansea never played to capacity houses - something which still rankles today - but perhaps that was not altogether surprising. There was no precedent for gauging the kind of support South West Wales would give to First Division football. Expectations were one thing, realism quite another.

On top of that Toshack's relationship with his players deteriorated. He lost their confidence and the magic touch which had carried Swansea so successfully from the Fourth Division to the top of the First.

The slump in the transfer market was another contributory factor. When Swansea tried to sell players they had bought for six-figure fees the bottom had fallen out of the market and they could not even give some of them away.

Of the £2.2 million Toshack spent on players the club recouped less than £800,000 from sales and, by the time they had been relegated to the Second Division, gates had dropped alarmingly from an average 18,200 to 11,600.

Swansea could not keep up the payments on Irwin, Latchford, Robinson, Stanley, Curtis and Kennedy and when the League slapped a ban on purchasing new players Toshack turned to the younger ones on the staff.

Despite a lot of optimistic noises, that policy never offered a long-term solution. The slide continued and it was difficult to predict just where and when it would stop.

New Hope, Old Problems

By the time the 1984-85 season started Swansea had fresh hope and a new manager in Colin Appleton, the man they originally wanted when Toshack resigned. It was rapidly developing into football's version of musical chairs. Out went Doug Sharpe, the chairman who persuaded him to join Swansea; in came Bobby Jones for a brief stay in the hot seat before he, too, quit to be replaced by Winston Rees.

At a time when there appeared to be more happening in the boardroom than on the field Malcolm Struel, still a director, was appointed chief executive, after ironing out his differences with Mr Sharpe. But the financial problems and the dissatisfaction among certain players in the dressing room was never far from the surface.

Rimmer, Robinson and Walsh were all told to go. Walsh and Rimmer refused, claiming the club had not honoured their commitments while Robinson complained with some justification that the club had not even bothered to thank him for suggesting a Stevie Wonder concert to raise funds for the club.

Swansea were told that major creditors Barclays Bank had first claim on the £250,000 compensation for the early retirement of Irwin, while the League were withholding levy payments to the club because Swansea still owed players who had left the club. The cash from the League levy pool was directed instead to Liverpool, Everton and Leeds to pay off transfer debts further underlining the gravity of

162/3. *left:* The fans go wild as Alan Curtis celebrates with Bob Latchford after scoring Swansea's fifth goal against former club Leeds. *right:* It's a goal and Jeremy Charles congratulates Ian Walsh.

Swansea's cash flow nightmare.

Walsh eventually agreed to move to Barnsley at a time when Swansea appointed three new directors to ease the worsening cash crisis: Mel Nurse, who started his career at the club; David Savage; and Harry Hyde, managing director of Diversified Products, the company which invested £50,000 to become the club's sponsors.

There was a little football, sadly all too little. Despite the efforts of Appleton the standard was poor and it was obvious early on that Swansea were heading for a third successive relegation season unless someone could stop the rot. Appleton, working under difficult circumstances, had used 22 players by mid-October when former England captain Gerry Francis was introduced in an effort to provide the experience and knowledge so desperately lacking. A month later, however, Swansea were dumped out of the FA Cup by non League Bognor Regis and even though the club insisted Appleton's job was safe the writing was on the wall. The crunch came on 4 December when Swansea were held at home by Spencer Works in the Welsh Cup. Three days later Appleton was fired after just seven months as manager and Chappell was back in charge insisting that he should have had the job in the first place.

The caretaker appointment lasted just eight days. Swansea moved for John Bond; and when Chappell claimed a lack of boardroom support he was promptly made redundant for going public with his criticism. Within days the backroom crisis was further underlined when former vice chairman Tom Phillips quit as a director after what he described as "thirteen months of bitter wrangling" to be followed soon after by Malcolm Struel who ended his 16 year association with the club by resigning both as chief executive and director. As two central figures in Swansea's rise and fall moved out, Bond swept in, determined to pin survival on experienced players

The wheeling and dealing had its effect. Swansea stopped the rot with a six match unbeaten run which eased the club off the bottom of the table but they still needed a point from the last match of the season against Bristol City to stay up.

They got it, thanks in no small measure to the experienced Rimmer, dropped just after Bond arrived but who responded magnificently when recalled in Swansea's hour of need. That obvious relief, however, quickly evaporated as Swansea embarked on a massive rebuilding programme against a background of growing financial unrest.

During the close season the cash crisis worsened and Rimmer, the highest paid player on the staff, confirmed long standing rumours that he loaned the club £20,000 to help pay for his £35,000 transfer from Aston Villa. Talk of a takeover continued throughout the summer but it was nothing more than that as Swansea limped from one deadline to another with directors dipping into their own pockets to pay wages.

164. An aerial shot of the ground and surrounding area.

165. Fifty-three days after quitting the management drama takes a new twist when Toshack is invited back with Chappell and Wyndham Evans as his assistants.

166. Despite a petition from the players the vacancy went instead to Colin Appleton who was sacked after seven disastrous months. This was his squad at the start of that 1984-85 campaign. *standing from left to right:* Colin Meldrum, coach, Chris Marustik, Wyndham Evans, Gary Richards, Roger Mullen, Michael Hughes, Jimmy Rimmer, Chris Sander, Pat McQuillan, Darren Gale, David Hough, Dudley Lewis, Les Chappell, coach. *front:* Tony Cottey, Dean Saunders, Neil Robinson, Colin Pascoe, Mark Hughes, Appleton, Nigel Stevenson, Jimmy Loveridge, Steve Mardenborough, Phil Williams.

167. New manager John Bond meets his board of directors, Doug Sharpe, Harry Hyde, Mel Nurse, Winston Rees, Dave Savage, Philip Owen and Peter Howard.

168. Among Bond's significant early captures was former Wales captain Paul Price being welcomed to the club by Chris Marustik, Steve Mardenbourgh, Colin Pascoe and Dean Saunders.

169. Goalkeeper Jimmy Rimmer, back at the club where he gained such popularity with a string of impressive performances on loan from Manchester United in 1973.

Dying Swans

There were the usual optimistic noises at the start of the 1985-86 season, but the worst day in the club's history was only a few months away.

The summer signing of Tommy Hutchison, one of the most talented and respected players in the game, certainly lifted the spirits of supporters who had grown tired of all the backroom bickering.

But problems were never far from the surface. Chairman Winston Rees and vice chairman Doug Sharpe resigned from office over boardroom differences and once again football was forced to take a back seat as a five-man management team took over the running of the club. The arrival of Chris Harrison, Gary Emmanuel, Colin Randell and Sean McCarthy almost went unnoticed as the full extent of the club's debts were revealed at a shareholders' meeting. Swansea, according to one director, were bleeding to death and faced being wound up by the Inland Revenue. A former director criticised the club for bad management and called for strong leadership.

The winding up petition was finally issued in September and within days the club was put up for sale triggering off a series of bizarre takeover moves which merely underlined the desperate depths to which Swansea had sunk.

In November the club won a stay of execution in the High Court. Swansea magistrates issued a distress warrant for non-payment of rates and when Swansea discovered that one of their prospective buyers was facing criminal charges the club was plunged into a new crisis.

Time had run out and on 20 December Swansea were finally wound up in the High Court by Mr Justice Harman who was scathing in his criticism over the way the club had been run. Grown men wept unashamedly as Swansea became the first club to fold in mid-season since Accrington Stanley 25 years earlier, and there seemed no way back for the club which had produced some of the game's finest players.

Alive Again

Behind the scenes the fight went on to revive the club. A Swans Aid campaign swung into operation overnight with thousands of pounds pledged in support and the promises kept pouring in once the Vetch Field management team, dubbed the Famous Five, successfully applied for a stay of execution on the winding up order.

Within days Swansea had been brought back from the brink and were now in the hands of a Special Manager, city accountant Jeffrey Payne.

In the new order there was no room for John Bond, the flamboyant manager who had kept the club in the Third Division with some rigorous team surgery the previous season. Instead Hutchison, the player Bond turned to in a bid to strengthen the playing side, was appointed caretaker player-manager charged with the same task as his predecessor. It was a daunting prospect and it became obvious early on that against a growing background of uncertainty where most of the key issues were being played out in the High Court, Swansea's hopes of staying up a second time looked extremely bleak.

No one doubted Hutchison's commitment but there was nothing to suggest any significant improvement. Swansea picked up few points and scored even fewer goals.

While Swansea's chances of surviving in the Third Division nosedived, the prospect of staying alive as a club rose dramatically with former chairman Doug Sharpe emerging as the likely saviour. The rival consortium in the Vetch Field boardroom backed down when Mr Sharpe's survival plan was given the official seal of approval and there was a further boost when the club's former directors agreed to write off nearly half the debts. But there was still a lot of work to be done before Swansea's future was secured. Manchester United offered a helping hand in a fund-raising match which produced a packed house on an emotional night that prompted one life-long supporter at the game to send the club a cheque for £10,000.

While it underlined the depth of feeling that existed, Swansea still needed substantial support, but clearly were not going to get any from the county authority.

The pressure was eased a little when Swansea were given the green light by the High Court to complete the season, but the wrangling continued, particularly over the transfer of cash from the Swans Aid Fund, with Official Receiver James Pope acting as overseer.

Creditors finally gave the Sharpe package the thumbs up at a special meeting at the Patti Pavilion. They voted 10-1 in favour, Swansea's biggest and most important win of the season.

By then Swansea had been relegated and Hutchison quickly discovered that he was not going to get the chance to revive Swansea on a permanent basis. That job went instead to Terry Yorath, a mid-summer appointment which coincided with Swansea's release from the High Court on their tenth appearance.

It cost £450,000 to wipe the slate clean, more than £300,000 coming in a personal loan from Mr Sharpe. The club which died, and was later revived, was back in business. For the men who masterminded the survival plan, Doug Sharpe and his financial adviser, Glyn Hammond, and for the manager pledged with the task of putting the emphasis back on football, it was the dawn of a new era.

Club dies as High Court judge winds it up

SWANS—IT'S THE END

THE High Court decision means that Swansea have effectively played their last competitive match.

Swansea were due to face Walsall at Vetch Field tomorrow in a Third Division fixture while the reserves were due at West Ham for a Football Combination game.

"We have clarified the legal position and have been told that Swansea City have ceased to trade. On that basis they are

THE advertisement in last night's Post for the match

clearly unable to fulfill their fixture commitment tomorrow," confirmed Football League press officer Andy Williamson.

He added, "By not playing tomorrow Swansea would lose their membership of the League by default.

"The only way Swansea could play Walsall would be if a rescue act was concluded today. There is no way we want to nail down the coffin lid before every avenue has been explored, but it looks hopeless."

Although it is believed that Walsall have let it be known that tomorrow's game is off, director Mr. Harry Hyde said this afternoon: "We are investigating urgently every possibility of playing the game. As far as I am concerned the game is not finally off."

Directors meet

SWANS directors Dave Savage, Peter Howard, Harry Hyde, Mel Nurse and Bobby Jones in crisis talks at Vetch Field this afternoon.

170. How the *Evening Post* reported the High Court action which wound up the club.

By Bob Bryant

SWANSEA CITY FOOTBALL Club's fight for survival finally ended today in the High Court in London when the club was wound up.

It is the first Football League club to fold in mid-season since Accrington Stanley 25 years ago. And this afternoon a liquidator was visiting the club to take over its affairs immediately.

Despite the news Swansea's directors were not prepared to go down without a fight. The board was in emergency session seeking advice on whether it would be possible to appeal against the judge's decision. Possibly overturn it.

At this morning's 35-minute hearing, both the Inland Revenue and the Vetch Field REsidents' Association opposed any further application by the club for an adjournment into the New Year.

The judge, Mr. Justice Harman, listened impassively as the court was told how the club had made repeated appearances but failed to meet any of its obligations or promises.

Looking on in the public gallery stone-faced was club vice-chairman Mr. Doug Sharpe, who had been working up until the last minute in an attempt to find financial aid.

Counsel for the club intimated there was a possibility of £500,000 being injected into the Vetch via America, but the promises fell on deaf ears.

Summing-up, Mr. Justice Harman lashed into the club, saying their case has been "all promises, promises, promises".

He accused them of illegally using money destined for the Inland Revenue and refused a passionate plea that the club was part of the life of Swansea — a piece of social history.

"Perhaps I was unwise to allow a further five days after hearing the case on Monday," said Mr. Harman.

"But money has been deducted from wages and should have been held by the club to be paid to the Inland Revenue, not to be disposed of or misappropriated on who knows what by the company.

"This company has very bad debts, but its promises of future funds are very vague and extreme. I see no grounds to seek any further indulgence of this court. This is a bad case and I also refuse the club leave to appeal."

This now means that from this morning the club has ceased trading and will not be allowed to fulfil any further League fixtures. No date has been set for a liquidator to be appointed.

A shocked Mr. Sharpe and club solicitor Mr. Robin Kirby

● To back page.

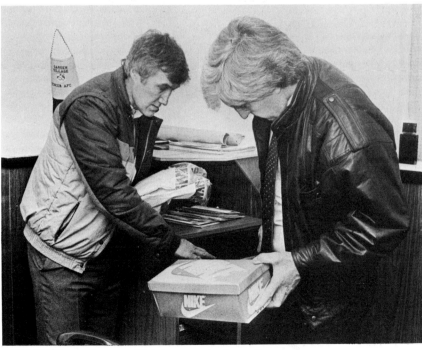

171/172. *above:* Tidying up before the gates are closed, John Bond and his assistant Fred Davies.
right: Shattered ... manager John Bond drives away from the club for the last time on the day the High Court issued the winding up order.

173. Locking up for the last time .. head groundsman Harold Woolacott.

174. Director Harry Hyde turns to PFA supremo Graham Taylor for help.

175. How can we save the club? A group of directors discuss the future with Swansea East MP Don Anderson.

176. Swans Aid swings into action and directors' wives and family lead the fight to keep the club alive.

177. Meeting the creditors. Doug Sharpe and his team of legal and financial advisers outline their survival package.

ALIVE AGAIN!

24 DEC 19

By PAUL CHAMBERT

SWANSEA CITY Football Club is today alive and kicking. A High Court judge yesterday exhumed the club from the grave when he granted a three-week stay of execution on a winding-up order.

Cheers for the Swans ... Mel Nurse and Peter Howard celebrate the stay of execution for the Swans outside the High Court in London.

Picture: Roy Tillett

Vandals slammed

VANDALS who daubed the home of Swansea City Council leader Councillor Tyssul Lewis have been slammed by Swans director Mr. Harry Hyde.

"The daubing was totally wrong and I do not think it was done by the true supporters of Swansea City.

"This kind of thing can only alienate the club and it's not the way we want our supporters to act.

"This was nothing more than senseless vandalism."

The Swans went into extra time today with a Receiver-Manager heading its business affairs and a new management for on the field.

Mr. Justice Scott granted the stay of execution in High Court Chambers in London on the application of directors Harry Hyde, Mel Nurse, Peter Howard and Dave Savage.

It was backed by former chairmen Doug Sharpe and Malcolm Struel.

The length of the reprieve was more than they had hoped for.

Offers

Mr. Hyde said: "We have achieved a miracle. We have rescued Swansea City from the dead. It was a million-to-one shot.

"But the judge in his wisdom decided that Swansea City could try again. "It was our package that rescued Swansea and no-one else's."

The "Famous Five" management team say they have bank backing for £200,000 and their "Swans Aid" appeal towards a £350,000 share issue to set up a new Swansea City '86 company has got off to a flying start.

They still see that as the best chance to keep League football in the city.

But Mr. Sharpe said his survival package was the most realistic. He had offers of financial aid from three Swansea businessmen towards his package, but would not say for how much.

"We will have to wait and see what happens in the next few days," said Mr. Sharpe.

Board

"But one thing is definite. I will not join the five. For me to become involved with them is not right for Swansea City Football Club."

Mr. Struel said: "I don't see the idea of a new company as being remotely viable. The best course is to keep the present company in being. I'm only interested in the survival of the club and I don't know whether I will be seeking a place on the board again."

● See 'Supporters Postbag' page 58; Get your act together — Back Page.

179/180. Alive again, and under new management, Special Manager Jeffrey Payne, appointed to run the club and Tommy Hutchison and Ron Walton, in charge of the playing side.

181. Doug Sharpe points the way forward to new manager Terry Yorath watched by directors Glyn Hammond and Mal Griffiths.

182. Out of the High Court's hands at last and time to celebrate for chairman Doug Sharpe and the playing staff.

A Helping Hand

Swansea, reprieved by their creditors and the High Court, were not making any rash predictions as the new season approached, despite the general euphoria at the club's continuing existence. In the event it was just as well.

With barely a month to prepare his team, Yorath moved quickly to sign full back Terry Phelan on a free transfer from Leeds, and re-engaged midfielder Gary Emmanuel, who had been released at the height of the club's financial crisis.

Colin Pascoe, Michael Hughes and Dudley Lewis all agreed to sign new contracts and there was a further boost when the unknown Ian Love came through a successful trial and was promptly offered a job. It proved a shrewd move. Love scored on his League debut on the opening day of the season, crowning a dream start when he struck the winner against runaway Champions Northampton to put Swansea top of the Fourth Division. Having seen their team beaten just once in the first eight matches, Swansea fans had cause to feel they were witnessing another revival. Sadly, it did not last despite important contributions from Pascoe, Lewis, Hutchison and the discovery of the season, central defender Andrew Melville.

Swansea tried to shore up the gaps by introducing loan signings Lyndon Simmonds, Paul Atkinson, Steve Lovell and Steve Kean but there were already doubts over whether the squad was strong enough to sustain a serious promotion challenge.

The loss of Love with a broken leg at Cardiff on Boxing Day was the first in a series of crushing blows from which Swansea never fully recovered. Although Swansea responded by increasing prices and inviting their fans to buy a player, most were still not convinced that Swansea would last the course even after top scorer Sean McCarthy had knocked Second Division West Brom out of the FA Cup with a last minute goal.

A managerial tug 'o war with Bradford, who wanted Yorath back as their manager, hardly helped the situation and when skipper Dudley Lewis was carried off with damaged knee ligaments in the next round of the Cup against Hull, the cause was virtually lost.

Even though Swansea completed the double over Northampton and enlisted the services of Huddersfield striker Paul Raynor a few hours before the transfer deadline, losing five of their last six matches underlined the side's lack of depth and consistency. Yorath's players could not even take advantage of a three point lift which they regained on appeal after the League docked them for not fulfilling a fixture.

Still, the foundations had been laid and Swansea, stiffened by the arrival of free transfer signings Alan Davies and Joe Allon from Newcastle, Jason Ball from Arsenal and £15,000 central defender Alan Knill from Halifax, had renewed cause for optimism.

Even the departure of the exciting Phelan to Wimbledon for £100,000 could not dampen spirits. Swansea found a ready-made replacement in Chris Coleman on their doorstep. Pascoe signed a new contract and the club got off to a flying start in their 75th season, winning 2-0 at Stockport on the day Tommy Hutchison made his 700th League appearance.

Sadly, the celebrations were cut short for player and club. Growing fears about the fitness of Hutchison were soon confirmed and his value to the side was not fully appreciated until his return six months later. Swansea, soldiering on without their influential midfielder, suffered five defeats in six games and were locked near the bottom of the table going into October.

Inevitably speculation over Yorath's future was never far from the surface but after a clear-the-air meeting with chairman Doug Sharpe, Swansea's fortunes improved, helped in no small measure by the creative Davies in midfield and a seven match scoring run from Allon.

By now Yorath had strengthened his squad by signing sacked Newport manager John Lewis, and the decision to stick by the inexperienced Coleman was providing another chapter in that long Swansea success story.

Just like Melville 12 months earlier, Coleman was proving the find of the season but Swansea attempts to stiffen the side even further were blocked when Cardiff turned down a bid for Alan Curtis.

Swansea were more successful with a £35,000 offer for Robbie James, another Vetch Field old boy, and the transfer from Leicester was completed two days after the club had been dumped out of the Welsh Cup by non League Merthyr.

Despite the introduction of the experienced James, and Love's remarkable recovery, a long succession of drawn matches underlined the worrying trend which kept the club on the fringe of the promotion race. Swansea hopes of stepping up the challenge were dealt a massive blow with the tragic news that goalkeeper Michael Hughes had to quit at 23 because of a brain abnormality. For a replacement, Yorath turned to Tottenham and the untried Peter Guthrie who, at £100,000, was the most expensive non-League player. They were beginning to regret the decision until the new goalkeeper produced a memorable performance at Torquay where Swansea were hoisted into fifth spot on the strength of Davies' winning goal.

By then Swansea had sold Colin Pascoe to Sunderland for £70,000 to balance the books, and had signed Peter Bodak in his place for a small fee. With two crushing home defeats against Rochdale and

Tranmere and a third inflicted by champions Wolves at Molineux it was little wonder that so many were writing off Swansea's chances.

However, Allon's winner at Peterborough in a week when Yorath was confirmed as caretaker Wales manager, produced a 10th away win, beating the previous record set by the Swansea pioneers of 1920-21, to keep the dream alive.

Swansea finally made it to the play-offs beating Darlington on the last day of the season while Wolves were giving them a helping hand by beating rivals Leyton Orient at Brisbane Road. Swansea scraped in through the back door in sixth place, seven points behind Torquay and Scunthorpe which underlined how the new format, for all its plus points, no longer rewards the consistent teams.

But there were not too many dissenting voices at Vetch Field as Swansea first overcame Rotherham and then Torquay, backed in no small measure by the return of Hutchison, Melville and Coleman, the growing influence of Davies and the goal scoring ability of Sean McCarthy.

The returning striker scored seven goals in as many games, including four vital strikes, one in each of the play-off matches, as Swansea crowned what had been a largely undistinguished campaign by clinching promotion in an absorbing finale at Torquay where Guthrie, despite earlier misgivings, produced a superb performance when it really mattered.

183. Manager Terry Yorath in a triumphal mood.

184. We're on our way. Sean McCarthy turns away to celebrate after scoring the winner in the play-off semi-final with Rotherham.

185. That man McCarthy again, this time scoring in the play-off final against Torquay.

186. Singing in the rain. Fans wait to cheer their heroes.

187. Fans gather outside the ground, start of the bus route around the city streets.

189. Swansea's goal scoring heroes at Torquay, Paul Raynor, Sean McCarthy and Alan Davies.

190. Open top bus tour around the city: starting out
from the Vetch.

191. Waving to the fans.

192. Arriving at the Guildhall.

193. Club captain Robbie James emerges from the crowds at the steps of the Guildhall with his wife Karen and daughter Hannah.

194. Doug Sharpe thanks the fans for their support after the Lord Mayor, Councillor Howard Morgan had congratulated the club on gaining promotion.

195. Terry Yorath acknowledges the cheering fans.

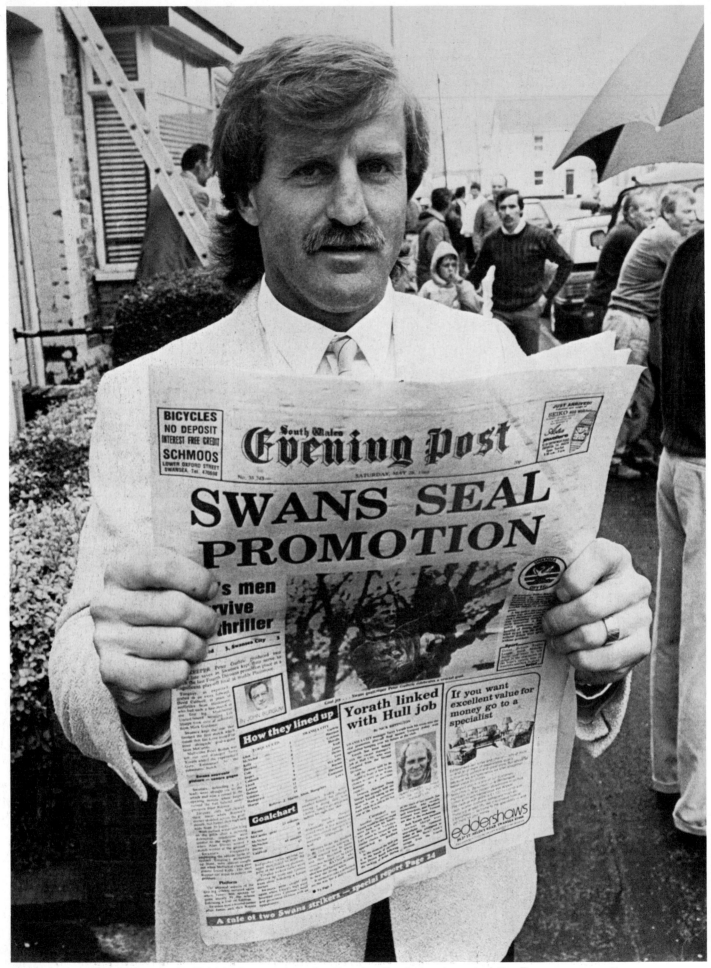

196. Club captain Robbie James gives the *Evening Post*'s treatment of the Torquay promotion decider the seal of approval.

197. Whisky galore. Terry Yorath collects his first manager of the month award.

198. Transfer deadline double: Paul Atkinson (*left*) on loan from Oldham and Paul Raynor from Huddersfield on a more permanent basis.

199. Colin Pascoe demonstrating the skills which prompted Sunderland to make a successful £70,000 offer scoring against Hereford in the Littlewoods Cup.

200. Being denied by Cardiff goalkeeper Mel Rees.

201.   Goalkeeper Michael Hughes being led off the field with concussion suffered in a pre-season friendly. Within seven months his brilliant career was cut short because of a brain abnormality.

202. Central defender Andrew Melville climbs above the Cambridge defence to head the equaliser, October 1987.

203. Terry Phelan, signed on a free transfer, sold for £100,000 to Wimbledon 12 months later.

204. Robbie James back on familiar ground after his £35,000 transfer from Leicester.

205. Replacement goalkeeper Peter Guthrie, who was untried, unsure, but
came good when it mattered.

206. Geordie-born striker Joe Allon, seven goals in as many games, two
short of equalling Ivor Allchurch's long-standing record.

207. The Swansea squad at the start of its 75th year. *back row, from left to right:* Joe Allon, Phil Williams, Chris Harrison, Keri Andrews, Alan Davies. *middle:* Paul Raynor, David Hough, Alan Knill, Michael Hughes, Andrew Melville, Jason Ball, Ian Love, Ron Walton, coach. *seated:* Sean McCarthy, Terry Yorath, manager, Dudley Lewis, Tommy Hutchison, Colin Pascoe.

208/209. The changing face of Vetch Field. How the skyline altered when Swansea built the East Stand which, as the then chairman Malcolm Struel discovered, caused considerable controversy among residents over the delicate question of compensation.

210. Promotion fever grips Swansea and the away support gets stronger. This shot was taken at Home Park, Plymouth.

Acknowledgements

The aim of this book was to compile the first pictorial history of Swansea City Football Club, appropriately celebrating its 75th anniversary.

It would not have been possible to achieve that aim without the considerable help of *Evening Post* chief photographer Len Pitson and his staff, John Corbett, Howell Davies, Mike Cleary, Alan Trethewy, Irwyn Morgan and Gareth Williams. In addition Gwen Griffiths, Tony Williams, Graham Harcourt (Printers) Ltd,. Bryn Matthews, the families of former players Ben Benyon, Ivor Brown, Billy Hole, Reuben Simons and Bill Whitehead, countless *Evening Post* readers and Swans supporters who have kindly loaned treasured family photographs.

Researching the early years was made easier by the unpublished material of Roy Morgan, excellent reference works by David Farmer (Swansea City 1912-1982), Bryn Matthews (The Swansea City Story 1912-1976), Tosh (an autobiography by John Toshack) and Karl Woodward (Western Mail).

Finally I would like to thank my publisher, Henry Hochland, and his staff for their kind help and guidance, my manuscript girls Lily, Barbara, Chris and Jean and last, but by no means least, my wife Sue for her patience and understanding. *Swansea City FC* was designed by Clive Hardy; cover by Lorraine Shaw; editorial by Liz Weekes.